Jesus' Gospel of the Kingdom:
A WOMAN'S PLACE

Jesus' Gospel of the Kingdom:
A WOMAN'S PLACE

There is no Sexism in Jesus' Gospel

VOLUME 3 OF 5

Thomas Z. James

XULON PRESS

Xulon Press
2301 Lucien Way #415
Maitland, FL 32751
407.339.4217
www.xulonpress.com

Paperback ISBN-13: 978-1-6628-3179-9
eBook ISBN-13: 978-1-6628-3180-5

Table of Contents

Dedication

This book is dedicated to the millions of modern Christian women around the world who have faithfully chosen to serve the Lord Jesus Christ while tolerating anti-biblical, un-Godly Christian sexism.

Introduction

THE TRUE CHURCH OF Jesus Christ has experienced several spiritual awakenings in past centuries, awakenings God has used to realign and even reset the spiritual priorities of the wayward Church. The Church is now amid still another spiritual awakening, one at least as broad in its scope and effect as any before it. In this one, God is emancipating Christian women to minister to Christians in every role available only to men in past centuries.

> This awakening is an awakening of women in Christian ministry. God is emancipating women from centuries of Church-imposed, yet biblically unwarranted, sexism to minister in every role available to men.

Over the centuries, God has used other spiritual awakenings to reform and transform both His true Church, and Western society in general. These past awakenings include such significant movements as the Protestant Reformation (1517+), the Great Awakening (1738+), and the Azusa Street Revival (1906+). In addition, the abolition of human slavery in Great Britain and the United States together comprised yet another spiritual awakening, albeit one having direct effects on both spiritual and secular arenas. Each of these awakenings, including the abolition movements, were used by God to realign His true Church more closely with His heart and general plans and purposes.

The current Women's Awakening, already global in its scale, is at least as significant in its impact upon global Christianity as any of these prior awakenings. Given its impact to-date and its virtually limitless potential, it is highly likely that future Church historians will regard this Women's Awakening as surpassing any to yet engage Jesus' true Church.

This awakening, as all those preceding it, is critically important to God and the progress of His Kingdom. It springs from the very depths of Jesus' own Gospel of the Kingdom, and God's own liberating love and compassion for the entire human race...love that includes both its male and female membership. Jesus' stated mission includes releasing captives from spiritual captivity, and women in traditional Christian ministry must surely rank among the most imprisoned captives on planet Earth. If you doubt this, just ask them!

Within the true Church of Jesus Christ, this issue directly affects the utility to the Kingdom of God of the female half of its membership, of their service to Jesus' Gospel, and of their God-given, supernatural enablements for ministry. Accepting Wikipedia's recent estimate of 2.3 billion Christians in the world today, this awakening therefore has the potential to dramatically and directly affect the 1.15 billion Christians who also happen to be women. And since women comprise a majority of truly active church membership in most Western churches, it is virtually certain that women are doing a large majority of actual ministry in the Church. Therefore, the net effect is that perhaps two thirds of all Church ministry has been restricted by the Transition View!

> Since women comprise a large majority of truly active church membership in many churches, the net effect is that perhaps two thirds of all Church ministry has been restricted by the Transition View!

To the extent that women are unjustifiably limited in their ministries, then their God-given enablements go either underused, or unused altogether, while they themselves are frustrated in their service to His Kingdom. Simultaneously, the needs which those unfulfilled ministries were intended go proportionately unmet. If even one person, male or female, is denied a single needed ministry act by such unwarranted restrictions, then satan wins that round, and the entire Body of Christ suffers its ripple effects. In effect, the army of God's Kingdom has imposed unnecessarily restrictive rules of engagement on the half of its soldiers who are women, to the collective detriment of the entire world.

> The army of God's Kingdom has mistakenly imposed unwarranted rules of engagement on the half of its soldiers who are women.

As a key part of its justifications for its sexism, the Church has ignored, heavily discounted or misinterpreted the multiple scriptural injunctions that oppose its gender-based restrictions on women in ministry. Just one example of this is found in the "body" metaphor used by the Apostle Paul to describe the proper function of the different parts of the Church. Within this metaphor, if one part of the Body of Christ rejects the help of its other parts, that body will be dysfunctional:

> *And the eye cannot say to the hand, "I have no need of you"; or again the head to the feet, "I have no need of you." (1 Cor. 12:21)*

In its immediate context, Paul was here emphasizing that every spiritual *charisma*-gift in a local assembly was equally necessary to its optimal operation. However, such gifts must necessarily include those gifts given by God to women as well as those given to men. By mistakenly restricting the use of spiritual gifts given to women, therefore, the Church at large has been doing exactly what Paul here advised it not to do, and has been doing so for at least the last nineteen centuries. The Church has, in effect, been saying to its spiritually gifted women, *"I have no need of you."* And it has been doing so while congratulating itself on its perceived faithfulness to scripture, unwilling to consider that its supporting justifications are mistaken.

> **Because it affects every Christian woman, and every man or woman to whom her ministry was denied, this issue profoundly affects every person on planet Earth.**

Only God knows how many potential female teachers or leaders have been told to be silent or have been denied the opportunity to share their divinely granted spiritual gifts and ministries with the Body of Christ, on the sole basis of their gender. Perhaps an even larger number of women have chosen a path of less resistance, and, in faithful obedience, have silently submitted to institutionalized, sexist, if anti-biblical, restrictions on their ministries. Because it affects not only those women so restricted, but also affects the collective eight billion humans on planet Earth who have been deprived of their ministries, this issue and its progress affect every living person on planet Earth.

> Although the Church at large has systemically imposed gender bias, it has done so in direct violation of God's ideal plan for women within the Body of Christ, and therefore within the Kingdom of God.

This book offers compelling, biblically based justifications for the emancipation of female Christian ministers from Christian sexism. It demonstrates that although the Church has systemically imposed this sexism upon its own membership, it has done so in direct violation of God's ideal plan for women within the Body of Christ. I thank our compassionate creator that His hand is guiding the ongoing Women's Awakening as it corrects and transforms this tragically longstanding mistake. Through this awakening, God is restoring women to the ministry roles He intended for them to occupy in His Kingdom from the very first days of creation. And God is doing so as an essential part of preparing His Church for the final harvest of souls in the ever-approaching End Times.

CHAPTER 1

Two Opposing Views...

THIS TOPIC IS MOST easily characterized and comparatively discussed using the perspectives of the two primary opposing views of the subject. The view most common among most traditional branches of Jesus' Church, both today and in past centuries, I characterize here as the "Traditional View." This view contends that God has and will continue to endorse effective sexism and gender bias in the Church and Christian ministry.

The opposing view, rapidly gaining broad acceptance across the modern Church, and revitalizing that Church in the process, I characterize as the "Kingdom View." This view contends that God has not endorsed such sexism at any time or in any venue in Christian ministries in the church age, whether in the past, present, or future. It is directly based on alternate interpretations of the same biblical passages used to support the opposing perspective, but ones which more accurately incorporate larger biblical themes of liberation and equality so vitally characteristic of the Kingdom of God. These interpretations rely upon the liberation of their more traditional interpretations from the toxic overprint of ingrained cultural biases of sexism so prevalent in virtually every secular and religious culture in the world.

The Traditional View

In modern forums, the Traditional View of women's proper roles in the Church has dominated most of the Church for most of church history, and this domination continues to the present day. This view is briefly summarized as follows:

> Traditional View – the view that her gender alone prohibits any woman from independently leading, teaching, or pastoring men, or exercising independent spiritual authority over men in any officially sanctioned capacity within Christian churches, ministries, or sectarian organizations.

Other than the mere handful of misinterpreted biblical passages which will be examined in later chapters, there are no official articles of faith, creeds, or confessions common to the widely variant groups who endorse some version of the Traditional View. Therefore, the beliefs of those advocates can vary widely while remaining true to the generalized description, above. In its most expansive dimensions, this group comprises most Protestant denominations and many independent Protestant groups, as well as Roman Catholicism and Eastern Orthodoxy.

Among the advocates of the Traditional View, to whom this book loosely refers as "traditionalists," the most stringent among them prohibit any woman from audibly speaking in any capacity in their public assemblies, for any authoritative purpose. In such groups, women are not allowed to teach or lead in any capacity, and certainly not from the highly visible pulpit on Sunday morning. Such strict groups require that women universally remain vocally silent from the start to the finish of every public gathering, wear head coverings and concealing items of clothing, grow their hair long, eschew makeup and all but the most modest jewelry, and defer to male leadership in every significant regard in all their Christian associations.

In contrast, more lenient traditionalists will allow women to speak in public assemblies, or to hold certain qualified leadership positions within their organizations. However, any such positions are typically required to operate under the authority and supervision of a male within the same organization. Such dependent positions might include a pastor over only women or children, as a Sunday School teacher of teenagers, or as a manager of administration, facilities, or childcare and hospitality programs.

One popular name used to describe one of the more accommodating forms of this viewpoint is the "Complementarian View." The name, "complementarian" was carefully chosen by its advocates to convey a "separate but equal" status to women, a status that nonetheless prohibits women from teaching, leading, or exercising spiritual authority over them. In this view, women are allowed to minister and serve, but only in roles that are supervised by men, or that complement the ministries of men under whom they serve. In the most lenient of these accommodations, women are allowed to pastor, evangelize, exhort, and even preach... but not teach. I leave it to its advocates to explain how the differences between those various endeavors are sufficient to permit women to minister in every way but teaching.

In practice, the Complementarian View confers no more functional parity to women in ministry than did the original phrase, "separate but equal" confer to the civil rights of Black Americans back in the day. Just as American Blacks were treated as second-class citizens by such "separate but equal" laws, so too are Christian female ministers treated as second-class ministers by the Complementarian View. Whether its label is the Traditional View, the Complementarian View, or any other superficially accommodating title, its functional reality is that any limitations on ministry based only on the gender of the minister comprise anti-biblical, un-Godly Christian sexism applied in the name of God. And while its advocates resolutely claim to base their views on scripture, the remainder of this book demonstrates that their justifications are altogether mistaken.

> The functional reality is that any limitations on ministry based only on the gender of the minister comprise anti-biblical, un-Godly Christian sexism in the name of God.

The Kingdom View

The opposing view, and the view advocated by this book, is referred to herein as the "Kingdom View." Another equivalent name used by other authors is the "Egalitarian View." This perspective, based upon Jesus' own liberating version of His Gospel of the Kingdom of God, contends that neither God nor Jesus condones or endorses Christian sexism in any Christian ministries or their leaderships, and that gender alone is therefore not a biblically justified criteria for limiting the permissible ministry roles of Christian women. Later chapters will reveal that both the Bible and church history demonstrate that God considers both men and women as equally eligible candidates for every independently functioning ministry office, position, and role in the true Church of Jesus Christ. Such positions include the biblical offices of apostle, prophet, pastor, evangelist, teacher, elder, and deacon, as well as managerial, administrative, or financial positions of authority.

Further, the Kingdom View advocates that the quality of God's leadership, guidance, wisdom, knowledge, and counsel is not dependent to any degree on the gender of any human vessel He might choose for its delivery. Correspondingly, the Holy Spirit is equally able to ordain, appoint, teach, lead, guide, and equip women as well as men, and each gender is equally able to perceive, receive, and impart such enablements. Consequently, both men and women should have equal and independent eligibility in the eyes of Christians, too, subject to their individual, non-gender-based qualifications.

> Kingdom View – the belief that God has placed no gender-based qualifications on Christian leadership and that both genders are equally eligible candidates on that basis alone for every leadership role in the Church of Jesus Christ.

God Endorses the Kingdom View

Regrettably, as the following chapters will demonstrate, the Traditional View is diametrically misaligned with God's perspective on the matter. He never intended for Christian organizations to limit the ministries of Christian women solely due to their gender. God created men and women equally in His image and granted to them equal authority and dominion in the Garden of Eden (cf. Gen. 1:26), and it was only the corruption of the Fall of Man that led to Eve's curse of submission to her own husband (cf. Gen. 3:16). To presume that the fallen condition of that curse comprises the normative status of women in the Kingdom of God is to completely misunderstand the key features of that Kingdom, and the marvelous extent of Jesus' restorative work in bringing that Kingdom to Earth, just as it is in Heaven.

Jesus' mission on Earth, of course, was to inaugurate the re-establishment of the Kingdom of God on Earth, just as it already pervades Heaven. The sexism that accrued to the fall of man (cf. Gen. 3:16) has no credible place in the marvelously superior Kingdom design to which Jesus came to restore mankind, and to which all Christians should aspire to walk within during their individual lives and ministries on Earth.

> The sexism that accrued to the fall of man (cf. Gen. 3:16) has no credible place in the marvelously superior Kingdom design to which Jesus came to restore mankind, and to which all Christians should aspire to walk within during their individual lives and ministries on Earth.

The correct perspective on this issue should necessarily align with God's revelations in the Bible. Since Jesus' primary mission in coming to Earth was to reveal the Gospel of the Kingdom of God (cf. Lk. 4:43), and since the overarching theme of the entire Bible is that same Gospel, the following chapters of this book rely upon a Kingdom-oriented perspective to interpret the relevant scriptural passages. In addition, Church history is reexamined from the same perspective. It is my continuing and most fervent prayer that the reader will consequently share my conclusion that the Kingdom View is God's true perspective on the subject.

CHAPTER 2

Setting the Stage for the Modern Conflict

THE ROLES OF WOMEN in independent leadership in both Christian and secular arenas have been significantly restricted for most of human history on the sole basis of Christian sexism.

> Sexism: (actions based on) the belief that the members of one sex are less intelligent, able, skillful, etc. than the members of the other sex, especially that women are less able than men (*Cambridge Online Dictionary*)

Even the most casual review of historical human organizations, both secular and religious, across every geographical and cultural boundary, will illustrate the near-universal sexist domination by men in most human organizations. However, in a truly historic development, the dramatic and divinely endorsed emancipation of women in both secular and religious arenas began about two-hundred years ago. This emancipation, while far from complete, is now well underway, and its rate of progress is even accelerating.

Like the secular societies in which they have lived, and for most of the first eighteen-hundred years of its existence, women's roles in the Church and in Christian ministry were quite heavily constrained by sexist restrictions that were not just unbiblical, but antibiblical, from the Kingdom View. For most of that time, female leaders, pastors, theologians, and academicians have been virtually nonexistent. For example, beginning in the New Testament, the gender of the original twelve apostles was uniformly male, as was the gender of most early church leaders. Centuries later, seminarians routinely study the writings of the Patristic "Fathers of the Church," (e.g., Irenaus, Tertullian, Athanasius, and Augustine) without the mention of a single "Mother" among them.

For the next thousand years, the organized Church in the West both prohibited women from ordination to church offices and from holding any positions of independent authority, while simultaneously preventing women from obtaining the education necessary for anyone to qualify for such roles. These prohibitions are reflected in many aspects of church life and culture, but none more so than in the fact that the Roman Catholics ordained no women to their priesthood during those many centuries. Within the Catholic faith in those years, the only church-approved occupation other than wife and mother available to women was that of serving as a nun or Mother Superior in a female-only convent.

Male domination within Protestantism continued the Catholic pattern, as is evident in the fact that all the leaders of the Protestant Reformation were men (Wycliffe, Hus, Luther,

Zwingli, Calvin, etc.). However, the Protestants, having rejected Catholicism, also rejected convents and their nuns. For Protestant women, consequently, the only church-approved occupation available to any woman, whether religious or vocational, was that of a wife and mother. Later, in the first few centuries following the Reformation, women as independent leaders were non-existent in every major Protestant and Catholic sect. While it is true that Catholics have beatified a small number of female saints (e.g., Mary the mother of Jesus, Catherine of Siena, Teresa of Avila, etc.), they have yet to ordain any woman as either a priest, bishop, cardinal, nor certainly as a pope. Correspondingly, any review of Christian literature during those many centuries reveals that it, too, is overwhelmingly dominated by male authors. This in turn was due, no doubt, to the prohibitions against women becoming literate during those same centuries. In general terms, most women were simply not given the opportunities, time or resources needed to become educated enough to read and write.

The Beginnings of the Modern Women's Awakening

The general absence of women in roles of Christian leadership began changing in the mid-nineteenth century, as the emancipation of women in both secular and religious arenas began a parallel, arguably co-dependent, development in the most progressive Western societies. A few bold women began rising up within the Church to answer God's call upon their lives, despite the deeply entrenched resistance to their presumption. These women comprise the earliest forerunners of what today has become the modern Women's Awakening. And they answered God's call to ministry in the face of resolute and determined resistance from most organized sects and denominations (resistance that is largely on-going) within the Church at large, as well as their secular societies in general.

Some of the most widely recognized among these forerunning women include:

- Elizabeth Fry (1780–1845),
- Dorothea Trudel (1813-1862),
- Phoebe Palmer (1807-1874),
- Hannah Smith (1832-1911),
- Mary H. Mossman (1827-1914),
- Catherine Booth (1829-1890),
- Elizabeth F. Baxter (1837-1926),
- Maria Woodworth-Etter (1844-1924),
- Pandita Ramabai (1848–1922),
- Aimee Semple-McPherson (1890-1944),
- Dorothy Day (1897–1980),
- Carrie Judd Montgomery (1858-1946).

As the earliest spiritual pioneers of the modern Women's Awakening, the deeply entrenched and quite powerful spiritual forces opposing their ministries insured that their efforts were restricted to the fringes of Jesus' true Church. In spite of such systemic sexism, the women listed above deserve far more respect and acclaim than they often receive in contemporary discussions. Any accomplishments on their part were achieved in the face of pervasively resistant cultural and religious sexism. Any modern student seeking to truly pursue first the Kingdom of God will greatly benefit from in-depth biographical studies of their courageous, even heroic, ministries in resources outside of this book.

Women Ministers in More Modern Times

Within the last fifty years, the Women's Awakening has been liberating increasing numbers of women to serve in positions of Christian leadership and authority. The movement is now encroaching into the very hearts of at least some of the major Protestant denominations. Some of the more recent female contributors, across the theological spectrum from fringe to mainline, include such women as Beth Moore, Kay Arthur, Joyce Meyer, Paula White, Cindy Jacobs, Elisabeth Elliot, Ruth Graham, Juanita Bynum, Michelle Corral, Audrey Mack, Jessica Maldonado, Patricia King, Clarice Fluitt, and Marilyn Hickey. The electronic age of television and the global Internet have dramatically enhanced the abilities of women to minister despite the deeply entrenched sexism so resistant to their efforts within the organized Church. Women now have multiple electronic platforms of communication from which they can effectively minister while free of sexist restrictions.

Today, multiplied thousands of women are dramatically equipping and strengthening the Body of Christ across its full breadth, and are doing so around the world. From their electronic platforms, and in whatever other venues they are given sufficient spiritual freedom and independence, their collective contributions are reaping bountiful spiritual fruit that is genuinely beneficial to the Church. Like previous spiritual awakenings, this Women's Awakening is ordained by God, on Earth just as it is in Heaven, and comprises yet another advance indication of the pending, if not imminent, arrival of Jesus' Second Coming.

> This Women's Awakening comprises a vital part of God's ongoing restoration of Jesus' own version of His Gospel of the Kingdom of God across His Church.

At its most profound level, and as its most compelling attribute, this Women's Awakening comprises a key element in God's ongoing restoration of critical features of Jesus' own version of His Gospel of the Kingdom of God. God originally created both man and woman in the Garden of Eden in His image...not two different images, one superior to the other, but one divine image. It is within that original, singular, holy image that men and women have equal spiritual stature, and share equal responsibilities, obligations, and privileges. It is to that original design that the entire Body of Christ is now being restored, as His Kingdom continues to encroach on Earth as it is in Heaven. And the ongoing Women's Awakening is a major avenue by which that encroachment is occurring.

The Abolition Movement as an Analogy

Throughout history, God has used secular influences to reform and correct His true Church on the occasions when its internal processes have failed to do so. In the ongoing Women's Awakening, God is in the process of doing so, yet again, to help awaken the Church regarding its mistaken perspectives on this topic. Substantial pressure in women's ministerial rights is being imposed on a resistant, modern Church by secular, societal influences that are leading such efforts despite the Church's resistance. As women gain stature and influence in such secular realms as business, finance, politics, and education, the modern Church is coming under increasing pressure to allow similar gains within its internal structures and organizations. The long-standing myths of women being somehow less capable than men of teaching or exercising authority over other people have been proven to be just that...myths.

Under ideal circumstances, secular influences should have no spiritual standing to comment upon matters internal to the Church. The Church correctly looks to God, and Him alone, for their doctrines since those doctrines so frequently oppose secular societal priorities. However, in those cases when the Church's doctrines violate God's true standards and are resistant enough to God's desired reformations via processes internal to the Church, God has, and will, use external secular means to initiate and encourage the needed reformation. God has repeatedly done so for His people throughout the Bible and has done so for the Church during the Church age, as well. A prominent example of God doing just that is the abolition of human chattel slavery in the ostensibly Christian cultures of Great Britain and America. In addition, these precedents also illustrate that consensus orthodoxy within the Church offers no guarantee, on the sole merit of consensus, that its official doctrines are correct, and are therefore divinely sanctioned.

It surely grieved Father God, and deeply so, that the influence of His true Church on both British and American societies was muted enough that the secular, legislative abolition of the horribly unjust, inhumane, and un-Godly practice of human slavery occurred over many decades. Regrettably, the organized Western Church tolerated and coexisted with human slavery in its various cultures for the first 1,800 years of its existence. Rather than the organized Church instigating abolition during those many centuries, it was the progress of democratic ideals in secular arenas (including the inalienable equality of all men) that finally matured enough for it to prioritize abolition.

Of course, far from everyone in even largely Christian societies are genuine Christians. Accordingly, non-Christians in those societies too often resist the priorities of God in favor of their own, typically un-Godly priorities. Consequently, at least parts of the collective Church should be credited with its determined persistence in the face of virtually systemic societal opposition to abolition.

God began the elimination of human chattel slavery in Great Britain and America, not through efforts of an organized Church, but by awakening small zealous groups of independent Christian abolitionists within their respective churches and societies. In addition, individually courageous activists such as Harriett Beecher Stowe and Sojourner Truth played highly prominent roles in the movement. Also, in some cases, local churches, with their spiritual sensitivities heightened to the authentic leadership of God Almighty, joined and supported the cause. Many of those churches provided spiritual and material support to abolition activities, support that was often illegal. One example is the support they provided to the so-called, "Underground Railroad", an ad hoc assortment of illegal escape routes and processes by which thousands of southern slaves were surreptitiously transported from the southern states to the free states in the northern USA.

In contrast, many local churches in America's southern states, and even entire denominations, had memberships who were either sympathetic to slave owners, or were slave owners themselves. The leaders of these churches managed to contrive and maintain sufficient consensus orthodoxy amongst themselves to officially oppose all abolition efforts. Rather than let the Holy Spirit guide them, their scholars had interpreted scripture with a pre-set bias that favored slavery, and that bias corrupted their interpretations. While modern standards of objective, biblical interpretation now consider their collective justifications to be grossly mistaken, those flawed interpretations were nonetheless the standard for many southern churches of that day. As this example so clearly illustrates, consensus orthodoxy on its own merit offers only a deceptively false protection against...deception.

While sympathetic elements of the Church contributed to the abolition movement, the ultimate victories of the movement occurred on secular fields of conflict. Subsequently, those secular victories then gradually reformed the resistant parts of the organized Church.

From a modern perspective, the progress of abolition was tragically slow in both countries. In Great Britain, their secular, legislative progress took place over a span of sixty-one years:

- first by a significant court judgement, the *Somerset Case*, in 1772,
- the legislative abolition of the slave trade by the *Slave Trade Act of 1807*,
- the legislative abolition of slave ownership itself by the *Slavery Abolition Act of 1833*.

Similarly, in America, the progress of abolition in legislative terms occurred over a time period of fifty-seven years:

- first by the nationwide abolition of the importation of slaves in 1808, by *The Act Prohibiting the Importation of Slaves*,
- next by the *Missouri Compromise of 1820*, that outlawed slavery in all territories west and north of the state of Missouri,
- next by the nationwide liberation of slaves in 1863, by the *Emancipation Proclamation*,
- finally, by the nationwide abolition of the slave trade and slave ownership in 1865, by its *Thirteenth Amendment* to its national Constitution.

Tragically, and with intentional toleration by large parts of the American Church, institutionalized racism persisted in America and many of its churches for another one-hundred years. Incredibly by today's standards, non-Caucasian minorities (Blacks, Asians, American Indians, etc.) were not given full rights as citizens in America until 1965. Incredibly, in a culture so otherwise proud of its technological advances, it was only a mere four years before Buzz Aldrin first walked on the moon (in 1969) that America eliminated its racist policies in official, statutory terms. Despite that success, the demonic spirit of racism is a major principality in the spiritual dimension and will likely continue to ply his nefarious work until the arrival of the End Times.

To its credit, much of the original abolition movement was nurtured and encouraged by sympathetic elements of the true Church, fully aligned with God's priorities of the unalienable rights and fundamental equality of all men. To its considerable discredit, however, far too many different elements of that same Church allowed both the foundational abuse of slavery itself, and for a full century afterwards, the associated abuses of statutory racism, to persist in society at large, and far too often even within its own ranks.

In the case of the modern Women's Awakening, God is demonstrating yet again, as He did in the case of the abolition movement, that He will use secular means to reform His true Church if its internal progress falls short of His divine intentions.

A Recent Example of the Contentious Nature of This Issue

The Traditional View has unjustly limited, or denied to, millions of female Christians the opportunities to release their God-given gifts in service to Jesus. The contentious nature of the Women's Awakening, and an insight into one such denial, was clearly demonstrated in a recent, public, and entirely unprovoked attack by one prominent male Christian leader upon a female Christian leader, described in the following account.

Among the more popular Christian teachers and authors of the current era, with a ministry focus in North America, is an American evangelist, Wanda Elizabeth "Beth" Moore (b. 1957). As of December 2020, Moore's personal bibliography included dozens of published books, Bible studies, training workbooks, and audio-visual presentations. Many of these works are available to the public on her website, located at *www.lproof.org.* In addition to her literature and presentations, Moore is a highly sought conference speaker, and has earned international acclaim and following for the high quality of her teaching. Having been called by God at a young age to her ministry, God has enriched the lives and ministries of millions of Christians of both sexes through Moore's ministry.

However, Moore's apparent popularity did not stop another prominent American Christian leader from disparaging Moore's leadership on the sole basis of her gender. Out of respect for his considerable positive contributions, and because his perspective on this topic serves as a proxy for thousands of like-minded church leaders, he will be referred to herein with the nickname of "Dr. No." His public and otherwise highly commendable ministry spans over fifty very prolific years, and he remains vitally active today. He, like Moore, is also an internationally acclaimed and widely followed Christian pastor, theologian, author, and conference speaker. He has published over one-hundred books, many hundreds of audio-visual presentations, and a wide range of Bible studies, commentaries, and articles. Dr. No is currently the lead pastor of a prominent mega-church located in one of America's largest cities.

From an administrative perspective, there has never been any professional or ministerial affiliation between Moore and Dr. No, other than the fact that both are prominent Christian ministers within the circles of North American Protestants. Neither has ever held any organizational authority over the other.

The unprovoked attack by Dr. No upon Moore occurred in a public church conference in early October 2019 at which Moore was absent. When Dr. No was asked to describe what he thought of Moore using only two words. Dr. No said she should "**Go home.**" His largely male audience, in apparent sympathy to his views, thought his comment to be humorous enough that many of them audibly laughed at his short response. While he was not specifically prepared to teach on the topic, Dr. No nonetheless made the statement without citing any objections to the relative doctrinal orthodoxy or biblical accuracy of her teaching. Rather, his only objection to her ministry was her gender. He did not consider her to be qualified for the sole reason that she is a female who has presumed to teach biblical truths in public forums having men in their audiences and doing so independent of any male oversight. In doing so, she had violated his own firmly held views on the issue. Lest he be misunderstood, he immediately clarified the meaning of his two-word declaration immediately thereafter by saying, "**There is no case that can be made biblically for a woman preacher – period, paragraph, end of discussion.**" Further, this unilateral, polemical attack by Dr. No was made without any provocation by Ms. Moore other than that of her presumption to independently teach men as a female.

Dr. No, at the pinnacle of his professional career as a respected Protestant leader, plainly considered the biblical case for women in public ministry to be definitively and permanently settled…in favor of the Traditional View. And he has much company in that regard, given that a significant majority of evangelical Protestant Christian leaders and educators hold similar views. Any one of thousands of like-minded, and equally dedicated and sincerely committed Protestant leaders would have made the same criticism of Moore, and for precisely the same reason.

As were the cases with human chattel slavery or the Protestant Reformation, however, consensus orthodoxy on any topic can be dramatically mistaken, while in the act of providing a deceptively false sense of theological security to its adherents. As was the case with both slavery and the Reformation, such consensus must be questioned when it contradicts not only more rigorous and thoughtful interpretations of the same Biblical texts used to support it, but larger biblical themes. As this book seeks to demonstrate, the Traditional View relies upon tragically mistaken interpretations of the Bible, just as the long-standing views of the Church regarding slavery and many key issues of the Protestant Reformation also relied upon quite orthodox and widely accepted interpretations of the Bible which are now considered to be mistaken (by Protestants, that is).

One Young Man is Alive Today Because Beth Moore Did Not "Go Home"

The dire need of the Body of Christ for every independent gift of ministry God has given to every believer, including specifically those given to women, is quite aptly illustrated by the following testimony. It recounts the miraculous resuscitation of a fourteen-year-old young man named John Smith (his real name), an event having a distinct link to the teaching of Beth Moore. Without Moore's public teaching ministry, it is virtually certain that Smith would not be alive today. The story received such wide acclaim that it was dramatized in the 2019 film, *Breakthrough,* written by Joyce Smith, directed by Roxanne Dawson, and produced by 20th Century Fox.

In the weeks prior to the event itself, the mother of John Smith, Mrs. Joyce Smith, had been attending a women's Bible study in a suburb of St. Louis, Missouri, USA. The group was using a workbook written by Beth Moore entitled, **Believing God** to guide their study. Among other teaching emphases by Moore in the workbook, one emphasis in particular made a singularly profound impression upon Smith. It was Moore's strong assertion in the workbook that Christians should offer every prayer with great boldness in approaching God, and with great faith and full confidence in God's willingness and ability to respond.

On January 19, 2015, while walking across a frozen lake with some friends, John broke through the ice and quickly drowned. Rescuers pulled his unresponsive body out of the water some fifteen minutes after he had submerged, and quickly took him to a hospital. A full sixty minutes after John had sunk to the bottom of the lake, a time during which he exhibited no vital signs, the attending physician in the emergency room of the hospital later recalled his bedside evaluation of John's condition in that moment:

> No spontaneous respirations. No heart tones. In essence, he was cold and he was dead. He was gone. (Dr. Kent Sutterer, "Breakthrough 2019," pg 1)

On the verge of declaring a time of death, the medical team stopped their considerable efforts to revive the boy, and respectfully called the dead boy's mother into the treatment room so she could say goodbye to her son. Having removed all other equipment, and with only an active heart monitor still attached to John's body, Joyce approached the operating table;

> (Joyce) walked up to the end of the bed and touched (Jn.'s) feet, which were the only part of his extremities that were uncovered. She recalls them being cold and grey. It was then that she began to pray out loud desperately. "'Holy Spirit, please come and give me back my son.' And within moments, he started to have a heartbeat," Joyce recalled. Her son John had been without a pulse for roughly an hour and the doctors had been trying to revive him for half an hour. (Ibid, pg 3)

Within mere seconds of her prayer, John's heart suddenly started beating again. Hearing the tones of the heart monitor, the stunned medical team immediately undertook to stabilize his condition. Even so, they considered his outlook to be extremely bleak. In full consideration of the lack of response in the first sixty minutes of his drowning, they fully expected major and irreversible damage to have already occurred in his brain and other vital organs.

In spite of this virtually hopeless outlook, fifteen days of steady, gradual improvement ensued, after which John had fully recovered:

> "Right at an hour with absolutely no life in his body whatsoever," says Dr. Kent Sutterer, "A complete healing. He doesn't have any seizures. He doesn't have any neurologic deficits, all the things that we expect in these things. Nothing. He's completely the same boy that he was before." (Ibid, pg 5)

As spectacular a miracle as was his initial resuscitation, equally remarkable was the fact that his brain and other vital organs were healed of every related side effect of his trauma. John Smith was the beneficiary of not just one, but multiple miracles. As proof of his complete and unqualified recovery, within several months of the drowning incident John had resumed regular attendance at his high school, his normal class and activity schedule, and his starting position on its basketball team. In witness to the spiritual impact of his miraculous resuscitation upon his life, as of this writing John is now attending college with the goal of becoming a Christian pastor, and is engaged to be married.

Regarding how Joyce Smith reacted to the sight of the life-less body of her son, far more common responses to a circumstance as certain as the witness of the cold, dead body of one's own child are frantic hysteria, irrational denial, or debilitating grief. In this case, however, Joyce Smith desperately asked God to intervene.

In multiple testimonial accounts, Joyce specifically credits the boldness of her prayer at the foot of John's operating table to the mindset and encouragement she received from Moore's teaching. While she had not called for the elders of her church to pray, had not anointed John's dead body with perfumed oil, had not asked unbelievers to leave the room, had made no dominion-based declarations, and had not exorcised any demons of death or infirmity, she undeniably energized sufficient faith to enable the resuscitation of her dead son. In addition, this was very likely one of those times in which Holy Spirit interceded for Joyce in groanings too deep for words (cf. Rom. 8:26). Although John Smith is alive and well today, there is no question that he would have died, and remained dead, on January 19, 2015, had Ms. Beth Moore followed Dr. No's advice, figuratively stayed at home, and thereby denied the gender-neutral, life-saving impact of her teaching to Joyce Smith.

CHAPTER 3

Hate Your Parents, Cut Off Your Hands, and Give Away Your Stuff

LATER CHAPTERS UNDERTAKE THE meaning of the biblical texts regarding the spiritual rights of women in Christian ministry. However, it is first worthwhile to review certain key elements of the process of accurate biblical exegesis, or interpretation. Some biblical passages are sufficiently clear as translated, are supported by sufficient contextual framing, and transcend all cultural distinctions, that they require relatively little analysis (e.g., *"Thou shalt not steal"*, Ex. 20:15). In contrast, however, virtually all of the key biblical passages commonly cited in the context of supporting Christian sexism require considerable textual and contextual evaluations for their accurate interpretation. This extra effort is required because the traditional interpretations of those passages are in apparent conflict with the larger context of the Bible and the revealed designs and intentions of Father God in general. Therefore, their reconciliation requires far more extensive evaluation than a simple reading of the texts themselves.

A determination of their literal meaning is certainly the first step in their interpretation. When I told a friend of mine that I was writing this book, his first response, and correctly so, was, "what does the Bible say?" However, if a shallow, literal reading is the only step taken, it will lead to the same mistaken interpretations of those passages as in times past and will allow similarly mistaken applications as before by those finding supposed biblical justifications supporting human slavery. We should certainly first ask, "What does the Bible say," right before we also ask, "What relevant contextual aspects should we consider as we interpret what the Bible says?"

> All the key biblical passages regarding gender bias are heavily influenced by cultural issues and therefore require considerable textual and contextual evaluations for their accurate interpretation. Their actual textual content is the first necessary element of their interpretation, but an evaluation of their context is equally important.

Textual evaluation comprises investigations of the specific vocabulary, verb tenses, grammatical structure, and other relevant linguistic attributes of the passage under consideration. Contextual evaluation, in contrast, is an investigation into the meaning of a particular verse or passage in relation to adjacent verses, passages, and chapters, analogous or relevant passages elsewhere in the Bible, larger biblical themes, and cultural or historical considerations. The combined application of these tools will significantly improve the interpretation of most biblical passages, and certainly any in apparent conflict with other Biblical passages and themes. To demonstrate how essential such tools can be, several illustrative examples are presented in the following sections.

Textual Evaluation Can Make a Significant Difference

For an example of the impact of accurate textual evaluation, the King James version (KJV) of the Bible translated the verse in Col 4:15 to say, *"the church which is in his house."* However, the pronoun used here in the original Greek manuscripts to describe in whose house the church is meeting is the Greek word, *autos* (Strong's G846), written here in the "genitive feminine third person singular" form of the word. Therefore, a more accurate translation renders the same phrase in English as *"...the church which meets in her house."*

Confirming this more feminine translation, this revised interpretation was used in more modern translations of this verse such as the NASB, NIV, Amplified, and Passion translations. It is only such a careful and conscientious textual evaluation as this that will enable an investigator to correctly interpret the other passages related to the subject of women's proper roles in Christian ministry.

Contextual Evaluation is Equally Critical

In a manner similar to that of textual evaluation, the various contextual aspects of any particular passage can have a profound impact on its proper interpretation. Context can take the form of the topical relationship of a passage to adjoining verses, passages, and chapters, the chapter's placement within its book, and a reconciliation of the verse to other related passages and to the Bible as a whole. In addition, it can also comprise various cultural and historical aspects of the original audience to whom the passage was addressed, and of the culturally influenced teaching methods used by the teacher.

Hate Your Mother, Cut Off Your Hands, Give Away Your Goods, and Handle Snakes

To illustrate how vitally important considerations of context can be, a hyper-literal interpreter of the Bible would be justified in advising his audience to:

- Practice genuine hatred of their mothers and fathers (cf. Lk. 14:26),
- Amputate their hands and feet, and pluck out their eyes (Mt. 18:8-9),
- Sell or give away everything they own (Mt. 19:21),
- Physically handle a few snakes and drink some poison (Mk. 16:17-18).

While acting upon rigidly literal interpretations of these verses would comprise nonsensical conduct to most of us, Church history contains multiple examples of groups who have done exactly such things. They did so because they failed to interpret the verses through appropriate contextual filters, while simultaneously ignoring the supernatural guidance of the Holy Spirit in their interpretations.

The statements of Jesus referenced above are only properly interpreted by considering that He often used the

then-common rabbinical teaching technique of hyperbole...
that is, using an extreme analogy to illustrate a less hyperbolic lesson.

In the case of hating mothers and fathers, therefore, contextual considerations reveal that Jesus' point was not that we should each literally hate our own parents, for that interpretation would violate the fifth commandment. Rather, Jesus' immediate audience, Dr. No, and every modern Christian, too, will consider that Jesus was here using hyperbole to illustrate that our love and devotion to God should supersede that of every human relationship in our lives, even to the degree of superseding our relationships with our own parents.

Likewise, rather than advising His disciples to physically mutilate their own bodies (cutting off hands and feet, and plucking out their own eyes), Jesus here used the extreme analogies of amputation and eye-plucking to illustrate the extreme commitment and resolve with which they should reject any sinful impulses in their lives. Similarly, in divesting their personal possessions, Jesus was instructing them to deliberately avoid any undue attachment to material possessions that might interfere with their devotion to Him. Finally, Jesus' reference to snakes and poison was a spiritual encouragement that, in the Holy Spirit, they would be amply enabled to defeat even demonic attacks posing as severe a threat to their spiritual well-being as venomous snakes and chemical poisons would present to their physical bodies.

Greet One Another With a Holy Kiss: Slaves Obey Your Masters

Regarding cultural context, biblical phrases that are over-printed with cultural influences were well understood by their original audiences, but are widely interpreted today with considerable latitude beyond their textual content. Two such examples are the following verses:

> *Greet one another with a holy kiss. All the churches of Christ greet you. (Rom. 16:16)*

> *Slaves, be obedient to those who are your masters according to the flesh, with fear and trembling, in the sincerity of your heart, as to Christ. (Eph. 6:5)*

Most modern American Christians will allow themselves ample latitude to greet one another with a holy kiss, or not, with no concern that they might be disobeying God if they refrain from the practice. Likewise, they will advocate that a slave has every God-given right to seek his own freedom, but to do so while treating his master with respect.

Just as it is necessary to consider text and context to accurately interpret and apply the verses about hating relatives, cutting off hands, and using holy kisses, it is likewise appropriate to do so when interpreting the verses alleged to govern women's ministry roles in church.

> Just as it is necessary to consider text and context to accurately interpret the passages about human slavery, hating relatives, cutting off hands, and greeting

someone with a holy kiss, it is likewise appropriate
to do so with the verses regarding women's ministry
roles in church.

Not even traditionalists rigorously committed to a literal
reading of 1 Tim. 2:12 would insist on literal readings and
applications of these passages (Lk. 14:26, Mt. 18:8-9, Mt.
19:21, Mk. 16:17-18, Rom. 16:16, Eph. 6:5), for to do so would
violate quite biblical, and valid, contextual considerations.
Extending that certainty to the subject of this book, I contend that, when similarly appropriate contextual considerations are applied to 1 Tim. 2:12 and other relevant passages,
the Traditional View is easily demonstrated to be false, and
the Kingdom View is shown to be God's own view.

The Greeks Were Paul's Target Audience

The accurate interpretation of any passage from one of
Paul's epistles will require a contextual understanding of
the specific culture of its targeted audience. The intended
audiences of each of the epistles largely comprised one of
three distinctly different cultures (Jewish, Greek, or Roman).
Each of these three cultures held a variety of attitudes
towards the civil and societal rights of women. As will be
evaluated in Chapters 4 and 5, the most compelling prohibitions against women in ministry, or at least seemingly so,
were written by the Apostle Paul to the Greek churches in
the cities of Corinth and Ephesus. His eponymous epistles
were obviously written to those churches, but so too were
his epistles to Timothy, a leader in the church in the Greek
city of Ephesus, and to Titus, a leader in the church in the
Greek culture on the island of Crete. In these epistles, Paul

was primarily addressing the appropriate behavior of Greek women, not Jewish or Roman women. A few Jews and Romans were likely also present in those immediate audiences, but Greeks comprised the clear majorities in both of them, and Greek cultural influences dominated their lives.

> In the epistles to the Corinthians, Ephesians, Timothy, and Titus, Paul was addressing the cultural behavior of Greek women, not women of other cultures.

While the strongly patriarchal Jewish culture of that day was overwhelmingly patriarchal and overtly sexist, and Roman culture as well, to a similar if somewhat lesser degree, women in Greek cultures were quite liberated by comparison. Greek Gentile women typically had been raised within the polytheistic Greek religion commonly observed across much of ancient eastern Mediterranean geography. Accordingly, in both Greek culture and religion, women were quite accustomed to exercising considerable authority over men in both secular and religious venues, and in both their public and private lives. For example, women often served as politicians, warriors, and even autonomous queens in the Greek societies of that day.

Greek women exercised such liberated behavior because many of the deities that dominated Greek polytheism were of the female gender (i.e., goddesses). Therefore, the human leaders that dominated many Greek religious sects were women. It was the attempted transference of this domination of women in Greek religious and secular culture into the new Christian churches that created the need for Paul to address the issue in the various passages discussed in the next two chapters of this book. And accurate contextualization of these passages is critical to their proper interpretation.

Don't Be Intimidated – God Himself Will Help You

Evaluations of text and context can be intimidating for lay Christians, the vast majority of whom have no formal training or education in theology, ancient languages, ancient societies and cultures, or history. However, a key element of the very good news of Jesus' complete Gospel of the Kingdom is that each of us, as individuals, can confidently depend upon the Holy Spirit to guide us into all truth:

> But when He, the Spirit of truth, comes, **He will guide sy-you into all the truth**; for He will not speak on His own, but whatever He hears, He will speak; and He will disclose to you what is to come. (Jn. 16:13, emphasis mine)

Jesus was here speaking directly here to each individual Christian, in every era of Christian history, when He directed the promise to "*you*". The pronoun He used here is the Greek word, *sy* (Strong's G4771), which, in grammatical terms, is in the form of the personal pronoun of the second person singular. He did not use a plural form of the pronoun. Therefore, Jesus directed this promise, not to a collective group of ecclesiastical conclaves, denominational boards, academic councils, or other general theological agencies convened to determine consensus orthodoxy. He made no mention of a requirement that our acceptance of any truth must first be processed through official theological filters.

Rather, Jesus made the promise of supernatural guidance by the Holy Spirit in doctrinal issues directly to you, to me, and to every other individual Christian. Jesus was here promising each individual Christian that the Holy Spirit would individually and personally lead and guide him into the spiritual truths necessary for his Christian success. And since Jesus said, *"all the truth,"* the word, "all" must necessarily include any textual and contextual evaluations needed to properly interpret and apply every applicable verse in the Bible, including any that might intellectually intimidate us. And, after all, Jesus said it Himself, so it is our obligation to then trust and believe that He will deliver on that promise.

Finally, in obedience to the following biblical exhortation, each of us is also obligated to make every effort, for ourselves, to accurately interpret the *logos*-word of God in our Bibles:

> *Be diligent to present yourself approved to God as a workman who does not need to be ashamed, accurately handling the logos-word of truth. (2 Tim. 2:15)*

Accurately handling the logos-word of truth (e.g., the Bible) necessarily includes our accurate interpretation of both texts and contexts of any given topic. By reason, therefore, Paul here encouraged every Christian to handle accurately even those aspects of text and context which might be intellectually challenging.

Even more importantly, however, to accurately handle the *logos*-word, we must simultaneously perceive and respond to the *rhema*-word of God contained within it, or we run the risk of missing the truths it contains:

> But He answered and said, "It is written, 'Man shall not *zao*-live on bread alone, but on every *rhema*-word that proceeds out of the mouth of God" (Mt. 4:4)

Jesus said here that every Christian is to *zao*-live on the dynamic, real-time, revelational *rhema*-word of God.

So which is it? Are Christians to *zao*-live on the *rhema*-word of God, as Jesus said here, or on the *logos*-word of God, as many Evangelical Bible teachers will contend? The answer is both: every Christian is to live by the more general *logos*-word as it is illuminated in his own life by the *rhema*-word, specific to his circumstances.

The very real danger in neglecting the *rhema*-word of God while exclusively pursuing the *logos*-word of God is that in so doing, Christians risk a repetition of the fatally legalistic mistake of the Pharisees:

> You search the Scriptures because you think that in them you have eternal life; it is these that testify about Me; and you are unwilling to come to Me so that you may have life. (Jn. 5:39)

While the *logos*-word of God is of vital importance, it cannot be fully comprehended or accurately applied without corresponding, supernatural enlightenment provided by the Holy Spirit. This enlightenment is the equally important *rhema*-word of God, specifically given to each Christian, and necessary to illuminate the more general *logos*-word as the Holy Spirit guides each Christian into all its truths.

Finally, if your favorite Bible teacher has ever presented the original Greek meaning of this or that word to you in his exegesis of a particular passage, he did so on the presumption that you are fully capable of comprehending the significance of such distinctions.

> Each individual Christian can absolutely depend upon the Holy Spirit to personally guide him into all truth...including any necessary textual and contextual evaluations.

When combined with Jesus' promise that the Holy Spirit will personally reveal all necessary truth to you as an individual, and God's provision for our comprehension of God's *rhema*-words, our remaining role in the process is to trust Jesus, to believe Him, and then to act upon the necessary truths as we perceive them. In fact, it is ultimately your personal responsibility to do so: any references you make to consensus orthodoxy or to the opinions of theological celebrities when standing before His Throne on your ultimate day of judgement will not be credited to your defense. Therefore, be confident of your own God-given abilities, and of the ability of the Holy Spirit Himself to supernaturally facilitate your spiritual education. With all due humility, hold up your head, stand up straight, and stride confidently into the following study of what the Bible genuinely teaches on this topic.

> Your role in the process of Jesus' promise to guide us into all truth is to trust Him, to believe Him, and then to act upon His promise to do so.

To be clear, I am not suggesting that each of us simply and completely disregard the opinions and views of generations of theologians, linguists, and scholars, and simply rely on our own individual interpretations in every Biblical matter. There can certainly be wisdom in many counselors under the right circumstances, and heresies are facilitated when someone relies too heavily on their own independent interpretations. However, I am suggesting that consensus orthodoxy by itself has proven to be a poor guarantor of truth (e.g., consider the poor advice given to Job by his three advisors, Eliphaz, Bildad, and Zofar). Multiple counselors can superficially agree, and seem to be right, when in fact they are very wrong!

From more modern times, consider the centuries-long, mistaken endorsement by consensus orthodoxy of such foundational subjects as human slavery, the false doctrines corrected by the Protestant Reformation, and most recently, the false doctrine of dispensational cessationism. Further, we should favor trusting in Jesus' promises more than fearing satan's deceptions, for we are to walk in firm, resolute faith in Christ and His promises, not in perpetual, choking and debilitating fear of satan and his deceptions:

And without faith it is impossible to please Him, for he who comes to God must believe that He is and that He is a rewarder of those who seek Him. (Heb. 11:6)

Jesus made significant promises to each of us as individuals that He would aid our personal comprehension of spiritual things. And if Jesus said so, we can not only safely believe it, but it is the very mission of every Christian on Earth to do so.

Christians should favor trusting in Jesus' promises far, far more than fearing satan's deceptions, for we are to walk in firm, resolute faith in Christ and His promises, not in perpetual, choking and debilitating fear of satan and his deceptions.

CHAPTER 4

Eight Secondary Biblical Misinterpretations

BIBLICAL VIEWS OF THE subject of Women in the Kingdom must necessarily rely upon biblical interpretations. For those views to be valid, however, the interpretations must themselves be credible. Regrettably, Traditionalists have mistakenly relied upon erroneous interpretations of allegedly relevant passages on this topic to support their views. Eight of these passages reviewed in the following chapter comprise:

- 1 Corinthians 14:34-35 (women are to keep silent church),
- 1 Timothy 3:1 (qualifications for a bishop),
- Titus 1:6 (an elder should be the husband of one wife),
- Ephesians 5:21-24 (wives should be subject to their husbands),
- 1 Corinthians 11:3 (the man is head over a woman),
- 1 Peter 3:7: (women are weaker vessels),
- Genesis 2:21-22 (Eve was formed from Adam's rib),
- Isaiah 3:11-12 (female leaders are a last resort).

A ninth passage, that in 1 Tim. 2:11-15, is significant enough that it requires the next chapter of this book for an appropriate level of evaluation.

1 Corinthians 14:34-35: "...*Women Are to Keep Silent in the Churches*..."

The Apostle Paul here explicitly states that women are to remain silent in public church meetings, and traditionalists sometimes cite this prohibition to support the Traditional View:

> **_The women are to keep silent in the churches; for they are not permitted to speak_**, *but are to subject themselves, just as the Law also says. If they desire to learn anything, let them ask their own* **_aner-husbands_** *at home; for* **_it is improper for a woman to speak in church_**. *(1 Cor. 14:34-35, emphases mine)*

Paul's statement here is seemingly straightforward in both its original Greek version and its English translations. If interpreted by relying only on its textual content, the passage can only mean that Paul considered it improper for any woman to utter even a single audible syllable of speech, in in any church meeting, under any circumstances. And such a prohibition would have applied regardless of whether the woman in question was speaking as a teacher or leader, simply making a public announcement, or merely asking for directions to the nearest exit. The passage continues to recommend that a wife, if she desires to learn, save any questions she might have for her own husband in the privacy of their home.

In contrast to a strictly literal reading, several textual observations readily disqualify this verse as a credible justification for the Traditional View. For example, v12:35 explicitly
states that the passage addresses only the disruption caused
by women who were audibly asking questions of their husbands during the progress of a public meeting and doing so
in a disruptive manner. A female teacher would be engaging
in an entirely different behavior, that of teaching the audience, not disruptively asking questions of her own husband
to educate herself. Therefore, the text does not support the
contention that Paul meant for the verse to apply to limiting
the speech of female teachers. For this reason alone, this
verse does not support the Traditional View to any degree.

Based on the text in v. 14:35, Paul's prohibition in v.14:34
only applies to a woman asking questions of her own husband. To extend that prohibition to any woman vocalizing
any statement in public under any circumstances, and to
women teachers in particular, comprises an application
of the verse entirely unwarranted by the text itself. While
the Greek word, *aner*, used in that passage can be translated as either "man" or "husband" (*aner*, Strong's G435),
the wording and context of this verse indicates that "husband" is the appropriate translation. Accordingly, Paul is
referring here to husbands, not to men in general. Therefore,
within the text of the passage itself, Paul was issuing a
restriction only regarding personal conversations between
wives and their husbands. That this was Paul's intended
application is further indicated by his statement in 1 Cor.
14:34 that women "...*are to subject themselves, just as the Law
also says...*", "*the Law*" here being a reference to God's first

mention of the topic in the original curse of marital submission put upon Eve:

> *To the woman He said, "I will greatly multiply your pain in childbirth, in pain you will bring forth children; yet your desire will be for your husband, **and he will rule over you**. (Gen. 3:16, emphasis mine)*

All the modern English translations agree with this interpretation, since they translate the Greek word, *aner*, here as the English word, "husband." Therefore, by virtue of the literal content of the text itself, the verse is altogether silent on any application of Paul's prohibition in this verse beyond the narrow limits of how wives should relate to their own husbands in public assemblies.

These two observations (Paul's prohibition does not apply to female teachers in the act of teaching and applies only to wives asking questions of their own husbands) are amply sufficient to invalidate the traditional interpretation of the verse. In addition, however, a rigidly literal reading of 1 Cor. 14:34-35 stands in direct contrast to the plain facts of Paul's previous exhortations for all Christians, including women, to speak in public congregational settings as they pray, prophesy, or speak in tongues (1 Cor. 11:5, 1 Cor. 12:1-31, 1 Cor. 14:1-6, 1 Cor. 14:29-31). Superficially, therefore, Paul apparently contradicted himself within the span of just a few verses, stating in 1 Cor. 11:5 and 1 Cor. 12:1-31 that women are to pray or prophesy in public meetings, while stating in 1 Cor. 14:24 that they are to remain silent. However, this apparent contradiction is no contradiction at all for the simple reason that a strictly literal, traditional application of 1 Cor. 14:34-35 to female teachers is invalid.

Paul specifically included all Christians, both men and women, *("... each one....")* when he exhorted them to share public words of prayer, prophecy, praise, teaching...yes, teaching..., revelation, tongues, or interpretation. Paul wrote the following passage, and indeed the entire epistle, to the general congregation at Corinth by addressing it to the *adelphos*-brothers at Corinth:

> *What is the outcome then,* **_adelphos-brethren_**? *When you assemble,* **_each one has a psalm, has a teaching, has a revelation, has a tongue, has an interpretation_**. *Let all things be done for edification. (1 Cor. 14:26, emphasis mine)*

The Greek word, *adelphos* (Strong's G80) is sometimes used in the New Testament to refer to male siblings or male ministry associates. However, in at least 225 times, it refers to all fellow believers, including both genders. And certainly in 1 Cor. 14:26, its context (e.g., *"...when you assemble..."*) demonstrates Paul was addressing the entirety of the general congregation, including both men and women.

Providing similar contrast, and unequivocal invalidation of the Traditional application of this passage, are the numerous biblical women genuinely ordained by God to speak in public assemblies. As reviewed in more detail in Chapter 6, these women include the prophetesses Miriam, Huldah, Deborah in the Old Testament, and Anna, the Samaritan woman at the well, the four daughters of Philip the Evangelist, Phoebe the deacon, Junia the apostle, Priscilla the teacher, and sixteen other women leaders identified in the New Testament.

> God's ordination of multiple women as judges, prophets, apostles, deacons, and church leaders throughout the Bible invalidates a rigidly literal reading of 1 Cor. 14:34-35.

While these multiple women were not all literally speaking *"...in the churches..."* they were nonetheless sharing the oracles and wisdom of God in public assemblies, thereby exercising spiritual authority over men, as ordained by God. As such, they would have been in at least a general violation of the traditional interpretation of 1 Cor. 14:34-35. For example, Anna certainly prophesied to both men and women, the Samaritan woman evangelized her entire town including its male citizens, Priscilla taught Apollos, and Paul had submitted himself to the spiritual leadership of Phoebe (each discussed more fully in following chapters). All these women were ordained by God to minister...to both men and women. On that basis alone, therefore, it is impossible for 1 Cor. 14:34-35 to mean that no woman should ever be permitted to exercise spiritual authority over men in a public assembly.

Clearly, however, Paul perceived the need to write the passage to address some problematic behavior. Considering cultural issues discussed elsewhere in this book, the most likely targets of the prohibition were Greek female converts who were presuming to import the domineering behavior they had enjoyed in Greek society and religious life into the

Corinthian church. The specific offending behavior, in context, therefore, was very likely a mere handful of outspoken Greek women exercising belligerent behavior as they disruptively asked questions during public assemblies.

From the perspective of the patriarchal cultures in which they existed, congregational meetings in New Testament churches were typically segregated by gender. The women typically sat in a different, more remote part of the same room as the men, sometimes in different, yet adjoining, rooms, or even altogether outside the main building. Given such separations, it would have been very disruptive to the larger meeting if even one couple tried to have a private conversation while speaking to each other across a room full of other people, and certainly if they did so while a meeting was in progress. If such an exchange became animated or even heated, then its disrupting effects would be proportionately amplified. Since modern church services are not typically so segregated, most churches ignore the restriction altogether. In most modern congregational meetings, each husband and wife sit together, and any question between the couple can be resolved with tactful whispers without causing undue disruption to the conduct of the larger meeting itself.

Further, traditionalists contradict a rigorously literal interpretation of Paul's prohibition every time they allow a woman to utter even a single syllable of audible speech in a public church assembly. Virtually every modern church, therefore, including the one pastored by Dr. No, universally allows women to audibly speak, even if only in private whispers to their own husbands and families. Therefore, every modern church and sect, including the one pastored by Dr. No, violates a rigidly literal reading of this verse. And it would be unreasonable, even untenably hypocritical, to ignore a literal reading of the verse by allowing any woman to audibly speak for any reason, but to then champion its literal content as a prohibition of female teachers.

Therefore, the collective consideration of the preceding points overwhelmingly invalidates the use of 1 Cor. 14:34-35 to support the Traditional View.

1 Timothy 3:1: *"If a Man Desires the Office of a Bishop..."*

A second passage sometimes cited by traditionalists is one in which Paul specifies the following qualification for men as candidates to be a bishop (also, elder, or overseer):

> *This is a true saying, **if a man** desires the office of a epis-kope-bishop, he desires a good work. (1 Tim. 3:1, KJV, emphasis mine)*

Traditionalists commonly use the omission in this verse of the mention of women seeking the spiritual office of a bishop to disqualify women for that office. Such an argument is one from silence, of course, and therefore lacking credibility on that basis alone. The verse itself is simply silent regarding women as candidates for the office of bishop.

Further, a simple textual analysis unequivocally discredits such a traditional interpretation of this verse. The Greek word translated by the scholars of the KJV into English as the word, "man" is the Greek word, *tis* (Strong's G5100).

This Greek word is more accurately translated into English as "anyone":

> "Tis": anyone, someone, a certain one or thing. An enclitic indefinite pronoun; some or any person or object. (from Strong's definitions)

The translators of other modern versions of the Bible addressed this issue with vocabulary more faithful to the original Greek word used in the passage, as follows:

> *Here is a trustworthy saying: **whoever** aspires to be an overseer desires a noble task. (1 Tim. 3:1, NIV, emphasis mine)*

> *The saying is sure: If **anyone** aspires to the office of bishop, he desires a noble task. (1 Tim. 3:1, RSV, emphasis mine)*

> *This saying is trustworthy: "If **someone** aspires to the office of overseer, he desires a good work." (1 Tim. 3:1, NET, emphasis mine)*

Therefore, had Paul meant to restrict candidates for bishop to only those of the male gender, he would have used vocabulary specific to that meaning. Paul most likely used the Greek word *tis* with deliberate intention, precisely because he did not consider gender as a viable exclusionary criterion for the office of bishop.

To strengthen their contention, traditionalists will sometimes note Paul's criteria in 1 Tim. 3:2 and 1 Tim. 3:12 and draw the inference that since Paul specified that an elder must be "...*faithful to his wife...*" or that a deacon be "...*the husband of one wife...*" that bishops, elders and deacons could therefore only be men. However, again, such a contention comprises yet another argument from silence, and invalid on that basis alone, since these verses also make no mention of the qualifications applicable to a female candidate.

While the Greek cultures of Paul's day were largely monogamous and official polygamy was frowned upon, extramarital sex by Greek men with temple prostitutes, concubines and slaves was commonplace. By virtue of Paul's mention of it, Gentile male candidates being considered for church leadership sometimes had more than one wife, wives likely acquired before the candidate had become a Christian. However, it was inconceivable that a single woman would have had more than one husband under any circumstance in those cultures. Therefore, while Paul felt the need to specifically address polygamy amongst male candidates for church leadership, he had no reason to even mention such a circumstance as a woman having more than one husband, because that circumstance was nonexistent.

The traditional interpretation of 1 Tim. 3:1 is even more substantially undone by Paul himself just a few verses later, when he implied that women could also be eligible to serve as bishops in the church:

> *In the same way, the women are to be worthy of respect, not malicious talkers but temperate and trustworthy in everything. (1 Tim. 3:11)*

Immediately thereafter, Paul then continues his review of a bishop's qualifications in verses 12 and following. That he mentions women in v.3:11, amid his larger review of the qualifications for bishops, contextually demonstrates that he viewed women as eligible candidates for such positions. To suggest that he interrupted his discussion on men's eligibility for leadership with a single, unrelated statement in 1 Tim. 3:11 about women's character unrelated to that discussion would untenably suggest that his thought pattern here, as well as that of the Holy Spirit who inspired this passage, were fickle, erratic, and unfocused, an entirely untenable assertion.

> That Paul included women in the midst of his discussion of the qualifications for bishops in 1 Tim. 3:1-13 confirms that he viewed women as eligible candidates for all such positions.

It is critical to note that 1 Tim. 3:11 occurs only a few short verses after Paul's prohibitive statement in 1 Tim. 2:12. It is clearly contradictory for Paul to prohibit women holding spiritual authority in 1 Tim. 2:12, only to then list them as candidates for the authoritative position of a bishop in the very next chapter of the same epistle. This apparent conflict is most reasonably resolved if the prohibition in 1 Tim. 2:12 does not apply to female teachers or leaders in the Church, so for this reason alone, the Traditional interpretation of 1 Tim. 2:12 is invalid.

In addition, as Paul lists the attributes of acceptable bishops in this passage, it is obvious by inspection that the attributes themselves are universal issues of personal character and morality and reflect no gender-based distinctions in themselves. According to Paul, bishops must exhibit the following character traits

- above reproach,
- temperate,
- self-controlled,
- respectable,
- hospitable,
- able to teach,
- not alcoholic,
- gentle,
- agreeable,
- not a lover of money,
- good family manager,
- mature in the faith,
- good reputation outside of church,
- worthy of respect,
- sincere.

Not one of the traits on the preceding list is unique to men, clearly indicating that Paul's only concern was the quality of personal character of a bishop, without any consideration regarding their gender. If the gender of a leader were as important to Paul as the Traditional View asserts, then it is more than merely curious that, having gone to such lengths to list the fifteen attributes of acceptable bishops on the preceding list, that he would somehow overlook the so easily discernable attribute of gender.

Therefore, in view of these observations, the only interpretation that honors the context of the entire passage of 1 Tim.

3:1-13 requires that Paul was including women as eligible candidates to serve as bishops. Therefore, 1 Tim. 3:1 cannot justifiably be used to restrict the participation of women in that ministry.

Titus 1:6: An Elder Should Be the *"...Husband of One Wife"*

In a passage bearing close similarities to the one discussed in the preceding section regarding bishops, Paul later specifies his requirement that polygamy disqualifies a man from being an elder in his letter to Titus:

> *For this reason I left you in Crete, that you would set in order what remains and appoint **presbyteros-elders** in every city as I directed you, namely, if any man is above reproach, **the husband of one wife**, having children who believe, not accused of dissipation or rebellion. For the overseer must be above reproach as God's steward, not self-willed, not quick-tempered, not addicted to wine, not pugnacious, not fond of sordid gain, but hospitable, loving what is good, sensible, just, devout, self-controlled, holding fast the faithful word which is in accordance with the teaching, so that he will be able both to exhort in sound doctrine and to refute those who contradict. (Tit. 1:5-9, emphasis mine)*

As they sometimes do with 1 Tim. 4:1, traditionalists will sometimes cite Tit. 1:5-9 and its reference to an elder as being *"...the husband of one wife..."* to indicate that Paul was thereby certifying that elders (Greek: *presbyteros* (Strong's G4245), could only be married, non-polygamous men. As is the case of bishops in 1 Tim. 3:1, and deacons in 1 Tim.

3:8, however, this is an argument from silence, and therefore without credibility on that basis alone. As was the case with 1 Tim. 3:2 and 1 Tim. 3:12, Paul was referring here to polygamy as a disqualification for male candidates, and not to any restriction on women in ministry. As previously noted, in the cultures of that day, only the eligibility of a man for service as a bishop, elder or deacon could possibly have been encumbered by a circumstance of polygamy.

As was the case in 1 Tim 3, Paul's list of specific character traits of an acceptable elder in this passage are clearly universal issues of personal character and morality and reflect no gender distinctions in themselves. According to Paul, an acceptable elder must exhibit the following character traits:

- above reproach,
- not self-willed,
- not quick-tempered,
- not addicted to wine,
- not pugnacious,
- not fond of sordid gain, but
- hospitable,
- loving what is good,
- sensible,
- just,
- devout,
- self-controlled,
- holding fast the faithful word,
- able both to exhort in sound doctrine and to refute those who contradict.

As was the case with the quite similar list of character traits for bishops and deacons in 1 Tim 3, each of the items on the preceding list are equally applicable to every candidate to be an elder, without regard to their gender. This interpretation is supported by the fact that Paul elsewhere uses the same Greek word, *presbyteros*, in a specific reference to women leaders:

> *Do not sharply rebuke an **presbyteros**-older man, but rather appeal to him as a father, to the younger men as brothers, the **presbyteros**-older women as mothers, and the younger women as sisters, in all purity. (1 Tim. 5:1-2)*

Paul's use here of the same word, *presbyteros*, to refer to both senior men and women in roles of leadership offers compelling support to the Kingdom view that his use of the same word in Titus 1:5-9 is a gender-less reference. Therefore, interpreting Titus 1:6 to connote a gender bias in the selection of elders is unjustified.

Ephesians 5:21-32: *"Wives should be subject to their husbands"*

Another passage sometimes cited to support the Traditional View is the following:

> *And be subject to one another in the fear of Christ. <u>**Wives, be subject to your own husbands, as to the Lord**</u>. For the husband is the head of the wife, as Christ also is the head of the church, He Himself being the Savior of the body. But as the church is subject to Christ, so also*

*the wives ought to be to their husbands in everything.
(Eph. 5:22-24, NASB, emphasis mine)*

The King James version of this passage uses both the words, "subject to" and "submit":

> ***Wives, submit yourselves unto your own husbands,
> as unto the Lord***. *For the husband is the head of the
> wife, even as Christ is the head of the church: and he is
> the savior of the body. Therefore as the church is subject
> unto Christ, so let the wives be to their own husbands in
> everything. (Eph. 5:22-24, KJV, emphasis mine)*

This verse describes Paul's requirement that a wife submit to her husband in issues of authority within their individual marital relationship. In so doing, Paul acknowledges and echoes the specific consequence put upon Eve after the fall of man (cf. Gen. 3:16), and the hard reality that the world at large continues to languish under the effects of that fall.

While this passage clearly speaks to the proper authority structure in a healthy marriage, it is altogether silent on the topic of the relationships of women in general Christian ministry to any other men in their lives or ministries. Therefore, it is only by use of an invalid argument from silence that the verse can be used to justify any gender-based restrictions of women in general Christian ministry.

It is very much worth noting that in Eph. 5:21, the verse immediately preceding Eph. 5:22-24, Paul made a related comment on the larger topic of Christians' attitudes towards each other within the Body of Christ:

And be subject to one another in the fear of Christ.
(Eph. 5:21)

Paul then extended the same general concept of loving, spirit-filled submission to the matter of the relationship of every Christian to his or her spouse...men to their wives, and women to their husbands. To reinforce the point, just a few verses later, Paul goes on to clearly establish God's preferred state of mutual submission of both the wife to the husband as well as of the husband to the wife:

> *So husbands ought also to love their own wives as their own bodies. He who loves his own wife loves himself; for no one ever hated his own flesh, but nourishes and cherishes it, just as Christ also does the church, because we are members of His body. For this reason a man shall leave his father and mother and shall be joined to his wife, and the two shall become one flesh. This mystery is great; but I am speaking with reference to Christ and the church (Eph. 5:28-32)*

One cannot correctly interpret verses 22 to 24 without properly framing them in the context provided by verse 21 and verses 28 to 32. Applying that context, this passage plainly teaches mutual submission, with spouses honoring and deferring to each other, rather than wives subservient to husbands. In full consideration of the influence of its immediate context, Eph. 5:22-24 does not teach that the ideal husband should exercise dictatorial, autocratic, and unquestioned authority over his wife. In a marriage, neither spouse is truly independent, but rather, each is co-dependent upon the other as the pair are in simultaneous co-dependence upon Christ. In their marital state, they truly are *"...one flesh..."*, forever spiritually conjoined with each other and with Christ, and are no longer separate individuals. In that state, as *"...one flesh..."*, neither has the latitude to simply do whatever they desire, without the informed and loving consent of both their spouse and Jesus. In particular, the husband must cherish and prefer his wife just as Jesus Christ cherishes and prefers the Church.

> A husband and wife truly are *"...one flesh..."*, forever spiritually enmeshed together, and are no longer separate individuals, so they should not try to function as individuals.

Further, within the three-way marital co-dependency just outlined (between Christ, a husband, and his wife), the passage in Eph. 5:21-32 enjoins a wife to submit only to her own husband, without any mention of a larger obligation to submit to any another man, male pastor, or other spiritual leader. She may be required to submit to appropriate male leadership external to her marriage for a host of other legitimate reasons (e.g., an employee to her supervisor, a student to her teacher, etc), but there are no such larger obligations revealed in this passage.

In addition, the spousal co-dependency within a marriage is conditional upon the submission of each spouse to the other. The mutual obligations to submit are degraded if either spouse violates his or her own obligation to submit to, love, and cherish the other. In the moment a husband becomes autocratic, physically abusive, emotionally abusive, unloving, or even despotic, he is no longer obeying

Christ, and his wife's obligation to submit to him is thereby nullified. Conversely, if a wife relates to her husband only through selfish manipulation, or via other abusive means, he is under no obligation to lay down his life for her.

Every marriage will undergo stress and compromise as the two spouses learn to live in three-way mutual love and submission between themselves and Christ. However, no blindly legalistic obedience to a misinterpretation of Eph. 5:22 can ever obligate a spouse to live within the pain, suffering, desperation, and hopelessness of a critically dysfunctional and abusive marriage. In such cases, qualified Christian marriage counseling will often serve to identify appropriate therapies and responses to such tragic circumstances.

The co-dependent submission just described should never be viewed as a curse of God-ordained subjugation and servitude, but rather as the heavenly blessing that God intended it to be. In the infinite wisdom of God, this arrangement creates a built-in, tie-breaking feature to every joint decision facing a married couple. In addition, each partner is thereby given that small liberating space in which they can submit to their spouse, thereby relieving themselves of the full weight of every decision and its incumbent responsibility and consequences. The submission of a wife to her husband, rather than being a curse so vilified by feminists, should be viewed as her opportunity to relax and share the weight and burden of family responsibilities with her husband.

Historically, overtly sexist Christian husbands have used Eph. 5:22 as a figurative cudgel to force their wives into strict obedience and compliance in any chosen area of disagreement. In the most tragic circumstances, such an interpretation has been used to justify the toleration of physical, sexual, and emotional abuse of the husband upon his wife. That such perverted logic has been used to convince a wife to endure such blatant evils, and to do so in the name of the God of love, mercy, and kindness, is an enormous and horribly unjustified distortion of God's truth. Abused wives should resist such evil, not tolerate it: they are to submit to God, not the devil masquerading as her husband (cf. Js. 4:7). It is no surprise that any sentient being would resent, resist, and even rebel against such abuse. God in no way endorses such dysfunctional behavior anywhere in the Bible, nor does He demand that a spouse tolerate such evil behavior for the sake of legalistic obedience to a single misapplied verse.

Instead of subjugating their wives and demanding their unquestioning obedience, husbands should treat their wives with the same gentleness, tenderness and understanding with which Father God treats the husbands themselves, and with which Christ loves His Church. They should love their wives with the same unconditional love with which they have been commanded to treat their neighbors (cf. Mt. 12:29-31). They should treat their wives with the same deference and consideration as they would treat Jesus Himself (cf. Mt. 25:40). The Apostle Peter recommended this approach in 1 Pet. 3:7 (evaluated in a following section), and for at least one very compelling reason: so that the husband would thereby avoid displeasing God and hindering his own prayers! Please refer to the more extended discussion of this verse in a following section.

Regarding major family decisions, both spouses should thoughtfully and objectively consider the counsel and opinions of their counterparts. In the event the two cannot agree, then the decision should be deferred until further prayer, fasting and counsel bring the two into harmony. In the event that a looming deadline demands an immediate answer before alignment can be reached, then in this circumstance alone has God given the husband the authority to be the tie-breaker and make the final decision.

Finally, the "great mystery" to which Paul refers in Eph. 5:32 is God's original co-delegation of equal dominion and authority to both husbands and their wives, as a reflection of the relationship between Christ and the Church. This delegation imposed no gender inequities or distinctions on their relationship (see expanded discussion in Chapter 9, following).

> Wives are to be subject to their husbands in the same manner as Jesus was subject to Father God... the required submission is for expediency of purpose, with no allowance whatsoever for neither the legalistic, autocratic, domineering, nor certainly abusive, control of the husband over his wife.

In summary, the passage in Eph. 5:21-32 has much to say regarding the proper authority structure in a healthy marriage, but is altogether silent on the topic of women in general Christian ministry. Its use in support of the general traditional view is therefore unjustified.

1 Corinthians 11:3: *"And the Man is the Head of a Woman"*

Sometimes cited in the context of the proper role of women in ministry is the following passage:

> But I want you to understand that Christ is the head of every man, and the man is the head of a woman, and God is the head of Christ. (1 Cor. 11:3, NASB)

It is critically important to observe that the verse states that, "the man is the head of a woman," but clearly does not state that "every man is the head of every woman." Just a few verses later, Paul confirms his intended meaning by referring to a single woman relative to a single man (ref. 1 Cor 11:9). To interpret these verses to mean that every man is the head of every woman, that is, has authority over her, and therefore no woman can assume authority over any man, not only exceeds its explicit textual content, but also comprises an irreconcilable conflict with the multiple times that God Himself appointed women to roles of leadership over men (see Chapter 7). God will never contradict Himself in His own scriptures, of course, so the apparent conflict is eliminated if one simply discards the Traditional interpretation that Paul meant to say that every man has authority over every woman.

A closer inspection of 1 Cor. 11:3 reveals that the Greek word *kephale* (Strong's G2776), translated in the NASB as the English word, "head," is more accurately rendered as the English word, "source":

> *But I want you to understand that Christ is the source*
> *of every human alive, and Adam was the source of Eve,*
> *and God is the source of the Messiah. (1 Cor. 11:3, TPT)*

Various scholars disagree on how the word, *kephale,* should be translated. However, the TPT version incorporates the meaning I believe is most consistent with the text and context of 1 Cor. 11:3, and explains its translation here in a footnote to the verse, as follows:

> Although the Greek word kephale, found three times in this verse, can be "head," it is used figuratively. It is not used in Greek literature or Scripture as "head over," "chief," or "ruler." To say that Christ is the head of every man means that he is the source of our life and faith as the head of the body of Christ. Christ is the "head" as in the head of a river. See also vv. 8-9, which support this. The source of the woman is man, for Eve was taken from Adam. The source of the Messiah is God, for he provided a virgin birth for Christ and formed his body and fulfilled the prophecies God spoke about him. (1 Corinthians 11:3, footnote 'c', TPT)

Therefore, Paul's use of the Greek word *kephale* in the preceding verse does not connote a generalized, universal *exousia*-authority of men over women, but is only a reference to Eve's positional source in Adam in the moment she was created.

Critical to this discussion is the observation that the New Covenant was intended to restore mankind to the liberated conditions existing in the Kingdom of God, the same conditions man had enjoyed in its first manifestation in the Garden of Eden. Christians, in their single-minded pursuit of the Kingdom of God (cf. Mt. 6:33) should aspire to live by the standards of the Kingdom of God, not by the standards of the fallen world. They are to aspire to righteousness, peace, joy and spiritual liberty in the Holy Spirit, not total-itarian, autocratic, slavish subservience. And since there is no such sexism in the Kingdom of God, discussed in more detail in later chapters, it is a mistake to so interpret this verse by unjustifiably assuming that such bias does exist.

Traditionalists will sometimes cite the next few verses in this passage as suggesting a subservient role for women relative to men:

> *A man ought not to cover his head, since he is the image and glory of God; but woman is the glory of man. For man did not come from woman, but woman from man; neither was man created for woman, but woman for man. (1 Cor. 11:7-9)*

Paul, in apparent anticipation of just such a misapplication, carefully reminds his readers just a few verses later that both men and women are equally codependent upon each other, precisely because both equally originate in Father God:

> *However, in the Lord, neither is woman independent of man, nor is man independent of woman. For as the woman originates from the man, so also the man has his birth through the woman; and all things originate from God. (1 Cor. 11:11-12)*

Paul plainly wrote here that neither man nor woman is independent of, and absolute master over the other, but that both should relate to each other as equal partners, with both subject to the authority of God Himself.

> Christians are to aspire to live by the standards of the Kingdom of God, not by the standards of the fallen world...and since there is no gender bias in the Kingdom of God, neither should there be any such bias in Christian ministries on Earth.

Therefore, in its proper context, when Paul wrote that *"the man is the head of a woman,"* he was referring to the proper authority structure between a husband and wife in their marriage (as he also described in Eph. 5:22-32, previously reviewed), and not to any other relationship between a man and a woman outside of marriage. This interpretation is confirmed by a footnote to the NIV translation of this verse (1 Cor. 11:3), that cites that an equally valid translation is *"...the head of a wife is her husband."* In addition, fully twenty-seven other English translations of this passage agree with the NIV translators in the content of their footnote on this verse.

In its larger cultural context, therefore, Paul's comments in this passage do not comprise a teaching on God's alleged design that every woman is to be subject to the authority of any man in the more public arenas of teaching, pastoring, prophesying, or public meetings. Rather, it was intended to correct the mistaken religious belief of his Greek audience that women were superior to men by virtue of their order of creation, and to encourage wives to submit to the authority of their own husbands within the confines of their marriages. Please refer to further insights on this cultural-religious context offered in the related discussion regarding the Greek goddess, Artemis in Chapter 5 of this book.

1 Peter 3:7: "...*giving honor unto the wife, as unto the weaker vessel...*" (KJV)

The title verse (1 Pet. 3:7) is sometimes used to support the generalized notion that women, as "...*weaker vessels...*" should therefore not be given spiritual authority over men in a position of public authority. However, a more careful examination of the verse and its context indicates it has a demonstrably different meaning and does not support the Traditional View. The NASB translation of the verse is as follows:

> *You husbands in the same way, live with your wives in an understanding way, as with someone weaker, since she is a woman; and show her honor as a fellow heir of the grace of life, so that your prayers will not be hindered. (1 Pet. 3:7, NASB)*

While the KJV translates the Apostle Peter's metaphor for wives as "weaker vessels", other modern translations apply different English phrases:

- *"Live with your wives in an understanding way, as with **someone weaker**"* (NASB),
- *"Be considerate as you live with your wives, and treat them with respect as the **weaker partner**"* (NIV),

- *"Live with your wives in an understanding way [with great gentleness and tact, and with an intelligent regard for the marriage relationship], as with **someone physically weaker**,* (1 Pet. 3:7, AMP).
- *"Husbands, you must in turn treat your wives with tenderness, viewing them as **feminine partners** who deserve to be honored,"* (1 Pet. 3:7, TPT).

Peter evidently considered women to be physically weaker than men. However, in giving that advice, Peter offered no comment on a woman's suitability for holding spiritual authority over a man. And while any such weakness may encourage a more belligerent person to use such that circumstance to assume and impose domineering authority, the verse itself implies no such thing. Quite the opposite is the case, in fact, as is made clear in Peter's more precise expansion of his meaning in the very next verse:

> *To sum up, all of you be harmonious, sympathetic, brotherly, kindhearted, and humble in spirit. (1 Pet. 3:8)*

The attitude of a husband towards his wife recommended here by Peter is not one of superior authority, oppression, and sexist domination. Rather, Peter advises here that husbands should relate to their wives with attitudes of gentleness, consideration, sympathy, thoughtfulness, harmony, kindness, and humility. Such attitudes carry no connotation of sexist restrictions on who should be in autocratic or dominating authority in such relationships, much less in public organizations. Therefore, based on the textual content of the verse itself, and as explained in the very next verse, this passage cannot be credibly used to support the Traditional View.

Also, Peter takes the idea of a gentle and mannerly husband one critical step further than Paul (cf. Eph. 5:21-32), however, and issues a warning that the prayers of an abusive and domineering husband will be hindered if he indulges in such un-Godly behavior. In so doing, Peter directly implied that God's displeasure in domineering behavior by a husband is significant enough that his prayers will be impeded or obstructed for that reason alone. Accordingly, any husband who demands autocratic, legalistic, and slavish obedience from his wife should be asked the question as to why he therefore prefers that his prayers be hindered!

> Any husband who demands autocratic, legalistic, and slavish obedience from his wife should be asked the question as to why he therefore prefers that his prayers be hindered.

In addition, the larger context of Peter's admonition in 1 Pet. 3:7 comprises part of his recommendations of the proper attitudes that should prevail in relationships between Christians and those whom society, culture, or God has put in authority over them. The passage advises that, to truly honor God, citizens should submit to their kings and governors, servants to their masters, slaves to their owners, and wives to their husbands. However, only in the special case of the relationship between a husband and wife does Peter advise that the one in authority exercise that authority with reciprocal attitudes of honor, consideration, deference, harmony, and kindness.

Not once in this passage (1 Pet. 3:7-8) does Paul refer to gender-specific ministry restrictions on female pastors, teachers, and other leaders outside their own individual marriage relationships. Not once does the passage say, or even imply, that women should not be permitted to teach or lead men, or to hold spiritual authority over men. In fact, the verse promotes functional gender equality by its reference to men and women as co-equal heirs of God's grace. Therefore, based on its larger context within the epistle of 1 Peter, this passage cannot be credibly used to support the Traditional View.

Genesis 2:21-22: Adam was Created First, After Which Eve Was Formed From Adam's Rib

Traditionalists have sometimes drawn the inference that since God created Adam first in the creation order (cf. Gen. 2:21-22), that their relative positions in that order relegates every woman to be subject to the authority of every man, or at least within Church leadership. As discussed in a previous section, Paul referred to this order of creation in 1 Cor. 11:7-9. And although for an entirely different purpose, Paul even specifically mentions this creation order in 1 Tim. 2:13 (see the related discussion in Chapter 5). However, the logic of using creation order to infer spiritual authority immediately fails, unless one is also willing to agree that stars, rocks, plants, and animals (cf. Gen. 1:11-25), created before Adam (cf. Gen. 1:26-27), have spiritual authority over men for the sole reason of their priority in the order of created things. In fact, angels preexisted mankind, but they exist to serve men, not the other way around (cf. Heb. 1:14, 1 Cor. 6:3). The order in which God created men, women, angels, animals, and the other elements in the world was governed by other priorities, but cannot be construed to impart any related hierarchy of spiritual authority.

If anything can be inferred from the place of a thing in the order of creation, one could argue that God's creation generally flowed from lower to higher orders (from rocks, to plants, to animals, to humans). Extending this trend, His creation of Eve as the final creation event could be construed to imply that women have superior spiritual authority to men. I do not agree with such an interpretation, but only use it to emphasize the irrationality of using creation order to infer any aspect of relative spiritual authority.

From the same passage (Gen. 2:21-22), others have proposed that because God used one of Adam's ribs to create Eve, this one-time physical dependency justifies her perpetual subjugation in authority to Adam, and thereby every woman to her husband, and then every woman to every man. However, just a few verses later, God Himself invalidated such an interpretation. He did so when He said that, as a married couple, the two would become, not a lop-sided pair in which the female was subservient to the male, but rather a pair so intimately conjoined as to form a single unit, forever united, inseparable and indivisible:

> For this reason a man shall leave his father and his mother, and be joined to his wife; and **they shall become one flesh.** (Gen. 2:24, emphasis mine)

In becoming "one flesh," the mysterious union of a husband and wife, as the relationship was originally created, forms a single spiritual unit in the eyes of God. The subsequent fall of man certainly interrupted God's perfect design by imposing upon Eve her subservience to her husband (cf. Gen. 3:16). However, within the perfection of the relationship between a husband and wife in which they were originally created, neither was given dominion over the other. Any Christian who is genuinely seeking first the Kingdom of God should also be pursuing the restoration of perfection in their marital relationship reflected in God's original design of it.

> Within the perfection of the relationship between a husband and wife in which they were created, neither was given superior authority over the other.

Finally, to assert that Eve's domination by her husband (cf. Gen. 3:16) is God's preference directly contradicts not only its identity as a curse rather than a blessing, but also contradicts God's original assignment of equal dominion when the two were first created:

> *And God said, Let us make man in our image, after our likeness: and **let them have dominion** over the fish of the sea, and over the fowl of the air, and over the cattle, and over all the earth, and over every creeping thing that creepeth upon the earth. (Gen. 1:26, emphasis mine)*

God said, "...*let them have dominion.*" God's explicitly stated design for the residents of His Kingdom is that men and women were originally created as equal partners, having joint and equal dominion on the Earth, with no indication of a higher order of dominion being given to Adam over Eve.

In summary, therefore, Eve's relationship to Adam, whether through the creation order or having been created from Adam's rib, has no bearing on their relative spiritual authority in the Kingdom of God.

Isaiah 3:11-12: Did Isaiah Imply That Female Leadership Should Only Be a Last Resort?

The following passage could be used to support the Traditional view by contending that it illustrates God's aversion to female leaders:

> *Woe to the wicked! It will go badly with him, for what he deserves will be done to him. O My people! Their oppressors are children, **and women rule over them**. O My people! Those who guide you lead you astray and confuse the direction of your (Is. 3:11-12, emphasis mine)*

Apparently, things would get so bad in the time prophesied here by Isaiah that women...*women,* if you can believe it... would take over and rule over the Israelites. Women!

The above passage could be interpreted to mean that Israel would become so rebellious towards God in some future time that a few rebellious women would throw off their subservient roles in society and assume control of the government. The application could then be made that if God presents the circumstance of women assuming political power as a negative consequence of the deteriorated nation of Israel, then He must therefore disapprove of women holding such authoritative roles in more prosperous times.

However, within the larger context of the Bible as a whole, God's earlier ordinations of Deborah, Miriam, and Huldah invalidate such an interpretation. In addition, a more contextually accurate interpretation can be made which accommodates not only those appointments, but the immediate context of the verse within the third chapter of the book of Isaiah as well. Earlier in the same chapter, Isaiah had spoken of how all the male leadership would be removed from the nation in the prophesied time:

> *For behold, the Lord God of hosts is going to remove from Jerusalem and Judah both supply and support, the whole supply of bread and the whole supply of water; the mighty man and the warrior, the judge and the prophet, the diviner and the elder, the captain of fifty and the honorable man, the counselor and the expert artisan, and the skillful enchanter. (Is. 3:1-3)*

According to this passage, men of every description will be "*...removed...*" and therefore simply absent altogether. Whether killed, enslaved, or incapacitated in some other way, their absence would mean they would no longer be on hand to fight, judge, prophesy, teach, or lead. Therefore, the most contextually accurate interpretation of Is. 3:12 is that the ranks of any qualified male leadership will have been so depleted that women will necessarily be drawn into the leadership vacuums so created. Those women will not displace male leaders in rebellious acts but will assume those roles because of a dire shortage of qualified male leaders. Therefore, the original passage is misapplied when used to infer that God disapproves of female leadership over men.

CHAPTER 5

The Primary Passage Supporting the Traditional View

EVERY MAJOR DOCTRINE OF the Church has several key scriptural passages on which it is based. This is also true of the Traditional View, but with one critical qualification. Having invalidated its alleged support provided by the eight passages in the preceding chapter, its support is entirely based on the following single passage:

> *A woman must quietly receive instruction with entire submissiveness. But **I do not allow a woman to didasko-teach or exercise authenteo-authority over a man, but to remain quiet.** For Adam was formed first, then Eve. And Adam was not the one deceived; it was the woman who was deceived and became a sinner. But women will be saved through childbearing—if they continue in faith, love and holiness with propriety. (1 Tim. 2:11-15, NIV, emphasis mine)*

Paul's statement here is seemingly clear and unambiguous, perhaps explaining why the Traditional View is so resolutely defended. A literal reading of this verse, without also evaluating its text and multiple contexts, quite directly supports the Traditional View. It is likely that Dr. No, for example, relied upon such a literal reading of this verse as justification for his unequivocal condemnation of the public teaching ministry of any Christian female, and Ms. Moore in particular.

However, if a literal reading is rigidly applied, this passage would also prohibit women from holding any public authority over adult males, or speaking to them in any public forum, including secular occupations outside the church. For example, a rigidly literal reading of Paul's demand that women must *"...remain quiet..."* would categorically prohibit Christian women from any of the following occupations, to the extent they would thereby exercise authority over men, would be teaching men, or would be speaking to men:

- Doctors, college professors, or military officers.
- Authors, lawyers, or judges.
- Store managers, business executives, politicians, or school principals.
- Journalists, news reporters, entertainers, or internet bloggers.
- Managers of charities and non-profit agencies.

Of course, Dr. No as well as every other careful interpreter will necessarily make considerable allowances when they interpret such explicit commands by Jesus as the ones about plucking out eyes and amputating hands or feet (cf. Mt. 18:8-9) or giving away all of one's material possessions (cf. Mt. 19:21). Likewise, they will also necessarily ignore a hyper-literal interpretation of 1 Tim. 2:12 when they allow women to be doctors, executives, politicians, or store managers ... or to utter even one audible syllable within their congregational church meetings.

Therefore, adherents of both Traditional and Kingdom views, Dr. No included, accommodate at least some interpretational latitude in their applications of 1 Tim. 2:11-15. Fundamentally, then, their disagreement is driven, not by the literal content of the verse itself, but by the differences in their interpretations of it. And if an interpretation is even the least bit subjective, and if its target is the only verse in the entire Bible that promotes a contested meaning having far-reaching impact (see next section), then those efforts should be conducted with the utmost care and consideration of all textual and contextual factors.

Accordingly, as the following sections demonstrate, a more rigorous textual and contextual evaluation of 1 Tim. 2:11-15 not only challenges the Traditional View but invalidates it altogether.

> Even Dr. No does not honor a rigidly literal interpretation of 1 Tim. 2:11-15, for, presumably, even he allows women to be doctors, executives, and politicians. Even Dr. No would certainly consider text and context in his interpretation of the passages about plucking out eyes and amputating hands or feet. In like manner, a more comprehensive textual and contextual evaluation of 1 Tim. 2:11-15 not only offers serious challenges to the Traditional View but invalidates it altogether.

The Entire Case for the Traditional View Rests Upon Only This Verse

The preceding chapter evaluated the alleged support for the Traditional View provided by the eight scriptural passages analyzed in that chapter. Hopefully, the reader agrees that those evaluations entirely invalidated that support for all eight of those passages regarding the Traditional View. Therefore, the entire case for the Traditional View effectively stands or falls upon the validity of its interpretation of just the single verse imbedded in the citation, above (specifically, 1 Tim. 2:12). And any doctrine based on only a single verse, and particularly one having such far-reaching impacts as the Traditional View, should be the subject of only the most careful evaluation to avoid misinterpretation. The question, "what does it say?", is certainly the necessary starting point of such an evaluation but is only the first of many related questions requiring consideration. Put another way, such a singular verse is only properly interpreted through the considerable context provided by the rest of the Bible, not the other way around.

> Such a singular verse as 1 Tim. 2:12 should absolutely be interpreted through the considerable context of the rest of the Bible, not the other way around.

This need is amplified by literally one billion times because the traditional interpretation of this single verse so directly and significantly limits the ministries of the half of the Church that is female. In so doing, it also deprives the entire two billion members of the Body of Christ, both females and males, of the gifts and ministries given by God Himself to the women so restricted.

Regarding the considerable weakness of having its justification in only one verse, and that verse subject to alternate interpretations, it is worth noting that every foundational truth of Jesus' Gospel of the Kingdom of God (e.g., the Church's doctrines regarding God, Jesus Christ, Holy Spirit, atonement, spiritual redemption and salvation, the baptism with the Holy Spirit, spiritual gifts and offices, heaven, etc.) is explicitly supported by multiple passages throughout both Old and New Testaments. Most were first prophesied, then demonstrated in Bible history, further expounded upon by Jesus or His apostles, again demonstrated by them, and finally prophesied for the Church age. God repeated these elemental truths multiple times and in a variety of ways precisely because He wanted to ensure that we correctly understand them.

God went to great lengths through multiple agents over thousands of years to repeatedly reveal and demonstrate each of the foundational elements of Jesus' Gospel. It is beyond merely problematic that the systemically impactful Traditional View is allegedly justified by this one, highly questionable interpretation of this one, single verse. No Old Testament prophets foretold it, neither the Old nor New Testaments modeled it, no apostles wrote of it, and neither Jesus nor His apostles taught it nor prophesied it (1 Tim. 2:12 excepted). If one knew nothing else about the subject, this glaring absence alone seriously undermines the Traditional View.

Regardless, that most curious singularity, by itself, comprises only an inferential argument. However, the Traditional interpretation of 1 Tim. 2:12 becomes wholly untenable when framed against its comprehensive textual evaluation, as well as the multiple passages and entire biblical themes which directly oppose it. Consequently, when viewed through both text and context, the Traditional interpretation of this passage is disproven altogether.

First Textual Comment on 1 Timothy 2:12

One widely respected Bible teacher and author, Andrew Womack, has observed that the King James translation of this verse prohibits a singular woman from teaching or usurping authority over not every man, but only a singular man. The KJV translation states the verse as follows:

> *Let the woman learn in silence with all subjection. But I suffer not a woman to teach, nor to usurp __authenteo-authority__ over __the man__, but to be in silence. (1 Tim. 2:11-12, KJV, emphasis mine)*

From the text itself, Womack interprets this verse to be a reference to only the manner in which a married woman should properly relate to her own husband in public settings. The verse is therefore altogether silent regarding the topic of women in general teaching or leading men other than their own husbands in general public ministry.

According to Womack's interpretation, therefore, the verse is silent regarding the Traditional View. If correct, then an interpretation so much more universal that it would prohibit any woman from teaching spiritual truths to any man cannot also be accurate.

Womack is far from alone in his interpretation of this verse. The NIV translation confirms Womack's interpretation in its footnotes on verses 11 and 12, footnotes too easily overlooked:

> *I do not permit a (**wife**) to teach or to assume **authen-teo-authority** over (**her husband**); she must be quiet. (1 Tim. 2:12, NIV, footnote alternates inserted)*

The footnotes to the NIV translation of this verse indicate that equally valid translations for the words translated as "woman" and "man" in this passage are "wife" and "husband." These alternates are substituted in the preceding citation of this verse by this author, for your convenience. Such footnotes are not simply casual afterthoughts by the scholars who translated the NIV, but instead offer alternative translations, equally valid as those more widely cited. Those translators understood that the ancient, koine Greek language uses the same word to refer to "man" as to "husband" (Gr. *aner*, Strong's G435). Likewise, it uses the same word to refer to "woman" as to "wife" (Gr. *gyne*, Strong's G1135). Therefore, which English words are chosen by the translators must necessarily reflect all available contextual considerations. In the case of 1 Tim. 2:12, the following sections will demonstrate that its contexts more strongly support Womack's Kingdom-honoring interpretation of this passage.

In consideration of the systemic domination of the Protestant Church by cessationism for the last five-hundred years, it is a virtual certainty that the translators of every modern translation allowed that bias to influence their rendering of 1 Tim. 2:12. In contrast, Womack's interpretation of the verse suggests that it was Paul's original intention for the verse to restrict the individual behavior of a wife towards only her own husband, and only in a public setting, but is altogether silent regarding the Traditional View.

> This verse refers only to the manner in which a married woman should properly relate to her own husband in public settings, and is therefore altogether silent regarding women teaching or leading men other than her own husband in general public ministry.

Second Textual Comment on 1 Timothy 2:12

From a related perspective, Womack's interpretation is supported by Paul's contextual shift to the singular tense of the words, "woman" and "man" (or "wife" and "husband") in 1 Tim. 2:12 from the verses immediately prior to it. In verses 9 and 10, Paul had just made several comments regarding proper attire for women in general, and he did so using the plural form of the word for women. His shift from plural "women" to a singular "woman" implies that Paul, in 1 Tim. 2:12, had changed the target of his comment from women in general to a single wife in relation to only her own husband.

Such an interpretation is consistent on a wider contextual basis with other passages such as Paul's admonitions that a woman should be subject to her husband (cf. Eph. 5:22-24).

And while Womack's interpretation can claim such external contextual support, the contrasting Traditional View has not a single other supporting passage to corroborate it.

In addition, Womack's interpretation is most consistent with Paul's subsequent explanation for the prohibition in verse 12:

> *For it was Adam who was first created, and then Eve. And it was not Adam who was deceived, but the woman being deceived, fell into transgression. But women will be preserved through the bearing of children if they continue in faith and love and sanctity with self-restraint (1 Tim. 2:13-15)*

Paul's observations here echoed the consequence put upon Eve after the fall of man, that she, as a married woman, would be subject in *exousia*-authority to her own husband, and only him (cf. Gen. 3:16). That consequence is entirely silent on the alleged larger application of the Traditional View, and any larger subjection of women in general to any alleged superior spiritual authority of men in general. Therefore, Eve's consequence was the reason that a woman should not usurp teaching authority over her own husband. And that consequence, specific to the relationship between a woman and her husband, has no bearing on the more general spiritual authority of men over women outside of an individual marital relationship.

Third Textual Comment on 1 Timothy 2:12

Another widely-respected pastor, author, and Bible teacher, Rick Renner, has noted that the conjunction of thoughts in the original Greek language in this verse is better translated into English as:

> **"I don't permit a woman to teach a man with the aim of usurping authority over him."**
> Renner, *Women in Ministry*, beginning at minute 58:20

According to Renner's interpretation, the acts of teaching and usurping authority are not separate and distinct behaviors, but are integral elements of the single offensive act of usurpation. Combining the observations of Womack and Renner, Paul was here prohibiting the act of teaching by a wife as a means by which she could impose domineering authority in public over her own husband. From this perspective, the verse is altogether silent on the more general topic of the Traditional View.

> Paul was here prohibiting the act of teaching by a wife as a means by which she imposed domineering authority over her own husband. Therefore, the verse is altogether silent on the more general topic of the Traditional View.

Fourth Textual Comment on 1 Timothy 2:12

When Paul here expressed his view of a woman exercising authority over a man, the word translated into English as "authority" is the Greek word, *authenteo* (Strong's G831). Its use in this verse is the only time that Greek word is used anywhere in the New Testament. This compares to the much more commonly used Greek word, *exousia,* translated as "authority," "power," or "right" in eighty-six applications in the New Testament. Examples of the use of *exousia* include the spiritual authority of Jesus as a teacher (cf. Mt. 7:9), the spiritual authority of disciples over demons (cf. Mt. 10:1), the political authority of Pontius Pilate over Judea (cf. Jn. 19:11) or Herod over Judea (cf. Lk. 20:20), the military authority over the centurion (cf. Mt. 8:9), and the creative authority of a potter over his working medium of clay (cf. Rom. 9:21).

Paul intentionally used the word, *authenteo* in 1 Tim. 2:12 to convey a different meaning than if he had used *exousia,* and this different meaning is critical to the proper interpretation of 1 Tim. 2:12. The following table emphasizes the differences in meaning between the two Greek words:

Exousia	*Authenteo*
constitutional, intrinsic	situational, improvised, extrinsic
ordained, sanctioned	usurped, appropriated
permanent, lasting	temporary, transitory
organized, structured	disruptive, unsettled, violent
general, generic	specific, particular
judicial, administrative	domineering, bossy, autocratic

Based on the differences in the preceding table, Paul was not here prohibiting generic women in all circumstances from teaching or exercising general, spiritual, ordained, *exousia*-style authority in ministry over men, such as she might apply in the role of an ordained and officially recognized senior pastor or teacher. If that had been his meaning, he would have used the more appropriate Greek word, *exousia*. Rather, Paul was here prohibiting a wife from teaching in a momentary exertion of *authenteo*-style dominance over her own husband, an authority that was temporary, usurped, belligerent, domineering, disruptive, and specific to its moment of application.

> Paul was here prohibiting a wife from teaching and thereby exercising *authenteo*-style dominance over her own husband with an authority that was temporary, usurped, belligerent, domineering, disruptive, and specific to its moment of application.

Fifth Textual Comment on 1 Timothy 2:12

In a fifth textual consideration of 1 Tim. 2:11-15, the following interpretation also reflects the recurring cultural dominance to which Greek women of that day had become accustomed, and with which they were probably disrupting teaching sessions in the church:

> One might wonder why Paul would have women learn at all if he believed they were never to speak or teach. As we will see, women do indeed teach, and Paul commends them on their work as they co-labor for the sake of the gospel. According to Witherington, 1 Timothy 2:11 tells women what they must do (learn), while 1 Timothy 2:12 states what they must not do at that time (teach): "The verb here, *epitrepō*, is present, continual tense. Paul does not say 'I will not/never

permit,' but rather, 'I am not [now] permitting.'"[7] The implication is that Paul's concern is not with women teaching, but with women teaching false doctrines, the primary concern of the entire epistle in context. **He is instructing the women to learn about their new faith at this time, not teach, because they need to be instructed regarding the faith so that they will be able to discern false teaching.** (Celoria, *Does 1 Timothy 2 Prohibit Women from Teaching, Leading, and Speaking in the Church?" pg 2, emphasis mine)*

Celoria's interpretation echoes the TPT translation of this passage:

Let the women who are new converts be willing to learn with all submission to their leaders and not speak out of turn. I don't advocate that the newly converted women be the teachers in the church, assuming authority over men, but to live in peace. (1 Tim. 2:11-12, TPT).

This interpretation explains how Paul could here place a limitation on newly converted females as teachers, while elsewhere acknowledging a considerable appreciation for the teaching abilities of more spiritually mature and educated women such as his Roman protégé, Priscilla. Please refer to the discussion of this remarkable female church leader, heartily endorsed by Paul in that role, in the following chapter.

By itself, therefore, this interpretation invalidates the use of 1 Tim. 2:11-15 as support for the Traditional View.

In 1 Tim. 2:12, Paul Was Moderating Their Expression of Usurped Class Superiority...Not Their Gender-Based Spiritual Authority

In the immediate context of the second chapter of 1 Timothy, Paul had previously advised women to dress more conservatively:

> *Likewise, I want women to adorn themselves with proper clothing, modestly and discreetly, not with braided hair and gold or pearls or costly garments, but rather by means of good works, as is proper for women making a claim to godliness. (1 Tim. 2:9-10)*

As Celoria notes, below, the assumed class superiority of the Greek women, acted out in both their behavior and their dress, was likely the offense that caused Paul to write this passage:

> I perceive the main problem that Paul is addressing in this passage to be women causing disruption of the community's worship through their behavior, which includes their appearance and communication. The first aspect of this disruption is inappropriate dress. Some of the women were dressing elaborately, which may have indicated their class superiority within the culture, a superiority that would not be appropriate within the Christian church community. (Ibid, pg 1)

Within the larger context of the entire second chapter of 1 Timothy, therefore, Paul was not declaring a restriction on women as leaders with authority over men in general ministry, as traditionalists claim. Rather, Paul was trying to moderate the flamboyant dress and domineering behavior of the newly converted Greek women so as to facilitate a higher degree of decorum and proper order in their church meetings.

> In the context of the second chapter of 1 Timothy, Paul was moderating the flamboyant dress and domineering behavior of the newly converted Greek women in their church meetings, not restricting the ministry rights of every Christian woman.

The Cultural Impact of the Pagan Worship of Artemis

In addition to the preceding observations, the leading religion in Grecian Ephesus in that day was Greek Polytheism. Further, the leading deity in that religion in the region of Ephesus was the Greek goddess, Artemis (equivalent in Roman Polytheism to the Roman goddess, Diana).

According to the views of Greek Polytheism, Artemis was the mother of all creation. In addition, she was also worshipped as the goddess of childbirth and of the hunt. Among its related beliefs was that women were created before men in the creation order, and thereby held superior spiritual authority. Accordingly, pagan spiritual authority was therefore exercised by women over men in their worship of Artemis, and women dominated the human leadership within its human organizational structures.

> In the temple worship of Diana, the chief goddess worshipped by the Ephesian culture, it was most common

to have female leadership. For the women who converted to Christ, their only cultural context of worship
was that the women were the leaders. (TPT, footnote
to 1 Tim. 2:11)

To the discussion at hand, it was likely his attempted cor-
rection of this belief that explains Paul's later reference to
Adam's higher position in the order of creation relative to
Eve in 1 Tim. 2:13.

In addition to her primary identity as the mother of creation, Artemis was also worshipped as the goddess of childbirth. Accordingly, most Greek women highly revered her
for that reason alone. The mortality rate of Greek women
in childbirth in that era was tragically high. Accordingly,
many Greek women would seek the protection of Artemis
by arranging to give birth in Ephesus in hopes that their
close physical proximity to the goddess and her temple
would earn the favor of Artemis in their greatest time of
need. Paul's reference (in 1 Tim. 2:15) to surviving childbirth through a properly directed faith in the protection of
the Christian God is very likely his attempt to correct this
false, pagan belief among the Greek converts at Ephesus.

Given the preceding observations, the first inclination of any
female who had previously worshipped Artemis, having
been saved into Christ, would have been to import any
gender-based prestige and religious and cultural dominance into both their own marriage as well as their new
Christian associations in the emerging Ephesian church.
Paul therefore wrote 1 Tim. 2:11-15 to prevent any woman

so inclined from inappropriately superimposing such domineering authority, either upon her own husband or within
the church.

Did Paul Contradict His Own Prohibition?

Yet another challenge to the Traditional interpretation of 1
Tim. 2:12 is found in Rom. 16:1-2:

> *Now, let me introduce to you our dear and beloved sister
> in the faith, Phoebe, **a shining minister of the Church
> in Cenchrea.** I am sending her with this letter and ask
> that you shower her with your hospitality when she
> arrives. **Embrace her with honor,** as is fitting for one
> who belongs to the Lord and is set apart for Him. So pro-
> vide her whatever she may need, for **she's been a great
> leader and champion for many – I know, for she's
> been that to me.**" (Rom. 16:1-2, TPT, emphases mine)*

Paul stated here that Phoebe, a female deacon, had been a
spiritual leader to many, including himself (please refer to
a more extensive discussion of this passage in the section
on Phoebe in the next chapter). Most critical to the subject at hand, Paul here states that he had subjected himself to the spiritual authority of Phoebe. Therefore, either
the Traditional interpretation of 1 Tim. 2:12 is false, and
Paul was not therein prohibiting any woman from ever
holding spiritual authority over any man, or Paul himself
violated his own prohibition by submitting to Phoebe's
leadership in Rom. 16:1-2. Of course, Paul did not contradict himself, either here or anywhere else, so therefore the

Traditional interpretation of 1 Tim. 2:12 is therefore false on this basis alone.

> Paul himself had submitted to the spiritual authority of Phoebe, a woman, so either Paul violated his own prohibition as alleged by the Traditional View, or the Traditional View is itself invalid.

A Summary of Observations on 1 Timothy 2:11-15

Based upon the collective insights of the preceding sections, Paul was using this passage to moderate the public behavior of Greek women who were attempting to import their pagan cultural dominance into their Christian marriages, homes and churches. With this perspective, it becomes even more apparent that Paul did not intend to prohibit women from teaching under any circumstances. Rather, he was only prohibiting them from teaching with the aim of usurping unjustified authority over their own husbands in public church meetings.

> Paul, in 1 Tim. 2:12, was not prohibiting any Christian woman across the entire Church age from ever having teaching or leadership authority over any man. Rather, he was only prohibiting their teaching if it had the aim of usurping unjustified authority over their own husbands in congregational church meetings.

CHAPTER 6

God Endorsed Women Leaders in the Bible

EVEN THE MOST CASUAL review of the genders of biblical leaders reveals that most of them were males. This majority has been cited by some traditionalists as evidence that God prefers male leaders. These same traditionalists will acknowledge the presence of a few women leaders in the Bible, but heavily discount their significance relative to the Kingdom View based only on their relative infrequency of occurrence.

However, God does not make mistakes, have accidents, stumble into coincidences, nor does He allow insignificant historical anomalies outside of His ordained will to casually creep in and misdirect His preferred course for biblical history (cf. Ps. 33:11, Is. 46:9-11). This is particularly true for those leaders He Himself has called and ordained into positions of leadership (cf. Rom. 13:1, Ps. 75:6-7, Dan. 4:17). Consequently, every legitimate, righteous female leader in the Bible, both Old and New Testaments, offers a directly applicable precedent, is present by the willful design and endorsement of God Himself and thereby proves God's view is the Kingdom View.

> Every legitimate, righteous female leader in the Bible, both Old and New Testaments, offers a directly applicable precedent, is present by the willful design and endorsement of God Himself and thereby proves God's view is the Kingdom View.

If even a single woman in the Bible can be shown to have either taught or exercised authority over men, with God's clear ordination and obvious endorsement, then the case for the Traditional View is seriously weakened. If dozens can be found, then the Traditional View is altogether invalidated, and the Kingdom View is unequivocally demonstrated to be true. Accordingly, as reviewed in the remainder of this chapter, twenty-eight different women in the Bible can be shown to have exercised God-ordained, righteously beneficial spiritual authority over men. Sixteen of these women indisputably exercised authority over men, while the remaining twelve are likely to have done so. Honoring the fundamental immutability of God (cf. Mal. 3:6, Js. 1:17, Heb. 13:8), it is reasonable to conclude that if God endorsed women leaders, prophets, and teachers with authority over men in Bible times, He endorses women in such roles today.

> If even a single woman in the Bible can be shown to have either taught or exercised authority over men, with God's clear ordination and obvious endorsement, then the Traditional View is weakened. If dozens are found, then the Kingdom View is explicitly and unequivocally proven.

The following twenty-eight women leaders in the Bible are each reviewed in their own dedicated sections within the following chapter:

- Deborah, Miriam, and Huldah
- Queen Esther
- Anna
- Mary the mother of Jesus, Mary the wife of Clopas, and Mary Magdalene
- The Samaritan Woman at the Well
- Junia the Apostle
- Phoebe the Deacon
- Priscilla the Teacher
- Chloe, Nympha, Apphia, Lydia, and "The Chosen Lady"
- The Four Daughters of Philip the Evangelist
- Tryphaena, Tryphosa, Julia, Euodia, and Syntyche
- Eunice and Lois

There were certainly many other commendable women in Scripture, such as Rahab, Lydia, Tamar, Dinah, Hagar, Jael, Rizpah, Hannah, Abigail, Ruth, Naomi, Leah, Rebecca, Rachel, Elizabeth, and Tabitha (also known as Dorcas). Each is worthy of their own individual study, each offering something for our collective edification. For example, Rahab is cited as helping Israel conquer Jericho (Josh. 2-6), is an ancestor of Jesus (Mt. 5:5), and a model of faith (Heb. 11:31). Ruth, too, is an ancestor of Jesus, and is significant because she is among the most famous Gentiles to have accepted God and His people as her own. Further, as a member of Jesus' lineage, she thereby introduced Gentile blood into that lineage. Lydia is mentioned as a faithful convert who gave welcomed hospitality to Paul and Silas during their visit to Philippi (cf. Acts 16:14-15). However, while the contributions of these notable women were sufficient for God to record them in the Bible, they did not demonstrate explicit leadership over men, and they are therefore not reviewed in the following sections.

There were also unrighteous women leaders in the Bible who were evil in the eyes of God. For example, such women as Jezebel, Delilah, Potiphar's wife, Athaliah and Herodias are not evaluated here, as their legacies as leaders were distinctly ungodly.

Deborah, Miriam, and Huldah

Examples of explicitly recognized female prophets in the Old Testament include Miriam (cf. Ex. 15:20), and Huldah (cf. 2 Kings 22:14). In an extremely authoritative role, it was Huldah who both interpreted and certified the Torah, previously rediscovered by King Josiah (cf. 2 Ki. 22), as the divine scriptures that comprised Jewish Scripture, and have since become a foundational part of Christian Scripture. Miriam is celebrated as Moses' sister, a prophet and leader of the Israelites alongside Moses and Aaron (cf. Mic. 6:4), and the author of the song recorded in Ex. 15:20-21. Both positions held distinct authority over both men and women, so these authentically divine ordinations clearly demonstrate women having been given authority over men by God Himself.

In addition to Miriam and Huldah, Deborah was appointed by God to be both a judge and a prophetess (cf. Jdg. 4:4). Deborah's case is particularly germane because a judge over

Israel in her day held the highest level of authority over all Israelis, both men and women alike. The authority of such a judge was equivalent to the near-absolute supremacy as that held by a king in other societies of the time. In her dual role as both judge and prophetess, Deborah was not only in command, but spoke with the authority of God Himself when operating under her prophetic mantle.

> God's appointment of Deborah as both judge and prophetess over Israel by itself proves God's endorsement of women leaders.

In the case of Deborah, God clearly had no issue with the gender of the person He Himself had appointed to such a supreme position of authority. To then suggest that God later developed a change of heart and decided that every woman under the New Covenant was not eligible to hold such authority calls into question the very immutability of God that is so vitally intrinsic to His being and comprises the very bedrock of Christianity itself.

From another perspective, traditionalists with a mistaken dispensational bias have suggested that the authority structures evident in the Old Testament are not transferrable to the Church of Jesus Christ, operating as it does under the New Covenant. They will apply this assertion to those circumstances in which female prophets and judges were operative. They consequently argue that a female prophet or judge in the Old Testament provides no valid precedent for female leaders in the Church age. However, such an argument has only the false and easily refuted, extra-biblical doctrines of cessationism and dispensationalism to discount the presence in the Bible of the female apostle named Junia, the teacher named Priscilla, the female deacon named Phoebe, Philip's four prophetic daughters, or Joel's prophecy that "daughters" would prophesy in the age of the Church (Joel 2:28).

Further, the New Covenant is superior in every major way to the Old Covenant (cf. 2 Cor. 3:6, Rom. 7:6, Jer. 31:31-34), and especially regarding spiritual liberty (cf. 2 Cor. 3:17). For example, the many behavioral rules of the Mosaic Law were not nullified by the New Covenant but fulfilled by it (cf. Mt. 5:17). Paul referenced this newfound spiritual liberty in direct terms in the following passage:

> *All things are lawful for me, but not all things are profitable. All things are lawful for me, but I will not be mastered by anything. (1 Cor. 6:12)*

This is because the New Covenant moves the race of men closer to its comprehensive attainment of the Kingdom of God and the supreme spiritual liberties that comprise it, not further away from it. To contend that the New Covenant would be more restrictive on the spiritual liberty of fully half of the entire population of the Body of Christ would directly contradict this truth. Therefore, the New Covenant allows more spiritual freedom, rather than less, in its consideration and treatment of the ministry roles of women in public service.

Finally, dispensational cessationism is false doctrine of the highest order, a fact discussed in more detail in the last section of this chapter. It therefore provides a fatally flawed base of support for any attempt to invalidate biblical precedents of female leaders and teachers.

Queen Esther

The remarkable story of how God used a spiritually ordinary Jewish woman to save the entire Jewish nation from genocidal annihilation offers a strong demonstration of God's endorsement of the Kingdom View. I characterize Esther as spiritually ordinary because she was not ordained by God as a judge, prophet, teacher, or any other recognized office having spiritual authority.

Esther's story is described at length in the biblical book of Esther. Very briefly, at a time when the bulk of the nation of Israel was being held captive in the kingdom of Persia, God elevated an ordinary Jewish woman, Esther, to the status of a queen, by virtue of her attractive physical features. In that role, God then gave to Esther the opportunity, the ability, the assignment, and the motivation to save her entire people through her leadership. God could easily have accomplished the same purpose using a male protagonist through any one of multiple alternatively imagined scenarios. However, the fact that He used a woman instead of a male offers a clear and undeniable demonstration of God's endorsement of the Kingdom View.

Anna the Prophetess

Anna is the first prophetess identified in the New Testament, a title that by itself demonstrates God's endorsement of the Kingdom View. While her identification as such occurred before Jesus' resurrection, the simple fact that Brother Luke gives to Anna the title of "prophetess" in his Gospel account certifies the legitimacy of her title in the eyes of God:

> **<u>And there was a prophetess, Anna the daughter of Phanuel</u>**, *of the tribe of Asher. She was advanced in years and had lived with her husband seven years after her marriage, and then as a widow to the age of eighty-four. She never left the temple, serving night and day with fastings and prayers. At that very moment she came up and began giving thanks to God, and continued **<u>to speak of Him to all those who were looking for the redemption of Jerusalem</u>**. (Lk. 2:36-38, emphases mine)*

This passage demonstrates that Anna operated in her prophetic office by ministering to all comers, both males and females, by teaching about Jesus as *"...the redemption of Jerusalem."* While the text is silent as to the genders of those she taught, it is reasonably inferred that she spoke to both genders by describing her ministry as speaking *"...to all those who were looking...". "...All those..."* must necessarily include both men and women. Therefore, the most reasonable interpretation of the passage is that Anna was prophesying to both genders and was doing so with God's explicit endorsement.

In addition, it can be safely concluded that the Jewish Pharisees and the ordinary Jewish people together recognized Anna as a divinely appointed prophetess. If they had not so recognized her, the high degree of religious zeal they held for the sanctity of the Temple alone would have caused them to immediately expel her from its grounds, if not stone her to death outright.

From this single passage, the following conclusions are readily demonstrated:

- God endorsed female prophets in Jesus' day,
- Anna was one of those prophetesses,
- The Pharisees and the ordinary Jewish people acknowledged God's endorsement by accommodating Anna's prophetic operation,
- Anna revealed the oracles of God to both men and women.

Taken together, these conclusions unequivocally demonstrate God's endorsement of the Kingdom View by the mere presence of Anna the Prophetess.

Three Marys (and John)

In another remarkable instance of women displaying leadership in the New Testament, it was women, not men, who displayed courageous leadership as they braved ridicule, abuse, and physical abuse to attend and comfort Jesus in the hour of His crucifixion. The Bible reports that most of Jesus' many male disciples watched the progress of the crucifixion itself from a safe distance:

> *And all His acquaintances and the women who accompanied Him from Galilee were standing at a distance, seeing these things. (Lk. 23:49)*

However, one small group comprising three very courageous women (plus the Apostle John), stood at the literal
foot of Jesus' cross. They did so to be close enough to Jesus
to offer their empathy and consoling companionship to Him
as He suffered and died:

> *Therefore the soldiers did these things.* ***But standing by
> the cross of Jesus*** *were* ***His mother****, and* ***His moth-
> er's sister, Mary the wife of Clopas****, and* ***Mary
> Magdalene****. When Jesus then saw His mother,* ***and the
> disciple whom He loved*** *standing nearby, He said to
> His mother, "Woman, behold, your son!" (Jn. 19:25-26,
> emphases mine)*

Parallel accounts of this event reveal that a very belligerent,
raucous, and antagonistic crowd had gathered to cruelly
taunt and ridicule Jesus in his last moments. Such a crowd
could easily have turned its hatred and abuse upon any of
Jesus' followers who were close enough at hand. It is no
surprise, therefore, that most of the disciples stood at a safe
distance to avoid such abuse. In contrast, the three women
and Brother John were exposing themselves to the very real
risks of at least emotional abuse, and very likely personal
physical injury, in being so close to Jesus. The collective fear
of the disciples of persecution in the first hours after Jesus'
crucifixion was quite real, as reflected in their manner of
later hiding themselves away in a closed room:

> *So when it was evening on that day, the first day of the
> week, and* ***when the doors were shut where the dis-
> ciples were, for fear of the Jews****, Jesus came and stood*

in their midst and *said to them, "Peace be with you."
(Jn. 20:19, emphasis mine)

Of course, the boldness with which those same fearful disciples would later go on to evangelize Jerusalem and the world would not come until after their empowerment by the baptism with the Holy Spirit (cf. Acts 2:1-36, Acts 4:8-12).

In the hour of Jesus' execution, however, among His hundreds of disciples, only three women (and John) had sufficient love, compassion, and empathy for Jesus to overcome their fears of being verbally ridiculed and physically assaulted and abused.

Such an exhibition, displayed in the quite belligerent face of significant, tangible threats to their personal wellbeing, demonstrates the exemplary leadership provided by these women (and John) to the other fearful disciples of Jesus... including the other ten apostles.

Two Marys and Joanna

Another significant instance of women being given a preeminent leadership role by God occurred on the day of Jesus' resurrection. In this event, God chose to first reveal both the fact of Jesus' resurrection, and Jesus Himself in His resurrected body, not to Jesus' male disciples...but to several women. It was women, not men, to whom was given the marvelous privilege of being the first human beings in history to learn of the glorious fact of Jesus' resurrection. It was to women, not men, that Jesus Himself gave the supreme

honor and privilege of His first post-resurrection speech
and appearance in bodily form:

> *Now after the Sabbath, as it began to dawn toward the*
> *first day of the week, Mary Magdalene and the other*
> *Mary came to look at the grave. And behold, a severe*
> *earthquake had occurred, for an angel of the Lord*
> *descended from heaven and came and rolled away the*
> *stone and sat upon it. And his appearance was like light-*
> *ning, and his clothing as white as snow. The guards*
> *shook for fear of him and became like dead men. The*
> *angel said to the women, "Do not be afraid; for I know*
> *that you are looking for Jesus who has been crucified.*
> *"He is not here, for He has risen, just as He said. Come,*
> *see the place where He was lying. "Go quickly and tell*
> *His disciples that He has risen from the dead; and behold,*
> *He is going ahead of you into Galilee, there you will see*
> *Him; behold, I have told you." And they left the tomb*
> *quickly with fear and great joy and ran to report it to His*
> *disciples.* ***And behold, Jesus met them and greeted***
> ***them. And they came up and took hold of His feet***
> ***and worshiped Him.*** *Then Jesus said to them,* ***"Do***
> ***not be afraid; go and take word to My brethren to***
> ***leave for Galilee, and there they will see Me."*** *(Mt.*
> *28:1-10, emphases mine)*

Oh, glorious day! Oh, joy unspeakable! With angelic hosts
shaking the very pillars of heaven with their shouts of
"Praise! Glory! Halleluja!", it was Jesus, whose death they
had personally witnessed, who was not only standing in
front of them, but was speaking to them! To mere women!
It was just as the prophets had foretold, and just as Jesus

Himself had foretold! Their spiritual future was no longer in a state of utter collapse and ruin, but had been miraculously secured for all men, and all women, for all time! Hallelujah, and Glory to God in the Highest!

> God first revealed the single most spectacular revelation in human history to women, who then immediately taught it to men.

Those women could not then contain their excitement, the thrill of which was growing by the moment as the full realization of the world-changing impact of Jesus' resurrection took hold! Joy unspeakable, indeed! As quickly as they could, they relayed the most stunning revelation in all human history to the fearful and disbelieving male disciples hiding out in fear of their lives in the Upper Room. Those women were the first Christians in history to share the spectacular news of the glory, majesty, and supreme hope of our risen Lord with anyone:

> *And they remembered His words, and returned from the tomb and reported all these things to the eleven and to all the rest. Now they were* **Mary Magdalene and Joanna and Mary the mother of James; also the other women with them were telling these things to the apostles**. *(Lk. 24:8-10, emphasis mine)*

Thank God that the Traditional View had not yet taken root: thank God that Dr. No was not on hand to quench their spiritual fire, or to prohibit them from sharing their news. These passages demonstrate that these women chose not to "go home" and remain silent, but instead immediately shared that revelation directly with the fear-stricken disciples. Their excitement was so great that they did so in the face of the disciples' incredulity and considerable resistance to it (*"...But they did not believe the women, because their words seemed to them like nonsense." (Lk. 24:11)*).

> God's distinctive use of women in this account, the first time in human history when someone of either gender first shared the spectacular news of our risen Lord, unequivocally demonstrates that God has no aversion whatsoever to women teaching men.

Rather than go to their homes and wait to report the revelation through male channels to satisfy the rules of engagement alleged by the Traditional View, these women chose to report the news themselves. This act would have directly violated any sexist protocols, had any such protocols already been established by Jesus. However, in this event, God first revealed the single most spectacular revelation in human history to women, who then immediately taught it to men. God's distinctive use of women in this account unequivocally demonstrates that God has no aversion whatsoever to women teaching men.

One well-known modern evangelist, Mahesh Chavda, has emphasized this same observation:

> Sending women as (the first) personal eyewitnesses to the Resurrection challenged age-old prejudices and firmly planted a standard, establishing women as spokespersons and witnesses to the works of God. (Chavda, *The Hidden Power of a Woman*, pg 32)

It is critically important to note that, in every biblical case, when God does something for the first time that He later repeats, His first demonstration establishes a clear and singular precedent for all future repetitions. For example:

- every modern Christian is correctly inspired by David's reliance upon his faith in God to profoundly defeat the mountainous threat in his path named Goliath,
- every modern Christian is correctly inspired by God's use of a single man, the Apostle Paul, to evangelize the entire Near East,
- every modern Christian is correctly inspired by God's use of Jesus Himself to model the perfect spiritual life we are all to emulate.

In like manner, every modern Christian, regardless of his gender, should be equally inspired to zealously share the good news of Jesus' resurrection and atonement, in imitation of the excited example of Mary, Joanna, and Mary.

It is no coincidence that at least two of those three women (Mary Magdalene and Joanna) had traveled extensively with Jesus along with the twelve apostles (cf. Lk. 8:1-3). They had walked with and sat at the very feet of Jesus for several years, and had had the privilege of learning every major teaching of Jesus directly from the Master Himself. They were therefore as familiar with Jesus' teachings as the eleven apostles (Judas had not yet been replaced), and therefore equally prepared to comprehend and reveal the stunningly profound revelation of His resurrection to their more fearful brothers in Christ.

It is keenly relevant to note that the risen Christ later confirmed the relative equality and status of women in the Church when He rebuked His disciples for not believing their report:

> *Afterward He appeared to the eleven themselves as they were reclining at the table; and **He reproached them for their unbelief and hardness of heart**, because they had not believed those who had seen Him after He had risen. (Mk. 16:14, emphasis mine)*

While their unbelief in the testimony itself was here the target of Jesus' rebuke, certainly contributing to their unbelief were the ingrained cultural gender biases towards the women's report of Jesus' resurrection. Had that same revelation been given first to several males in their group, there is little doubt it would have been more readily received. And those gender biases were clearly considered to be unjustified by Jesus Himself in this passage.

Jesus could have told them, "Hey, I know they were only women, but you should have believed their report in spite of their gender." Instead, Jesus clearly expected them to believe their report, regardless of their gender...because their report was absolutely true, and because absolute truth is never, ever qualified by the gender of its spokesman. Jesus had absolutely no sympathy for their sexist bias, and particularly so because it caused them to doubt the women's first-hand testimony of the most significant event in world history. The truth of Jesus' resurrection was earth-changing news, and the gender of those first reporting it was completely irrelevant to its import and significance.

> Jesus' reproach of the disciples in Mark 16:14 illus-
> trates that the truth and relative importance of any
> divine revelation is wholly independent of the gender
> of the human vessel through which it is revealed, and
> is in no way compromised or devalued by it.

While only a speculation, I can easily imagine Jesus also giving a reproach to Dr. No similar to the one He gave to His own disciples. In such a speculative scene, Jesus would tell Dr. No to consider and apply the divine truths contained within the teaching of Beth Moore, rather than reject Moore's role in relaying those same divine truths simply because of his poorly justified disapproval of Moore's gender as a teacher.

The Samaritan Woman at the Well

Chavda also observes, just a few pages later, that God chose, not a man, but the Samaritan woman at the well (cf. John 4:7-42) for a similar distinction, one which offers an undeniable violation of the Traditional View:

> <u>This Samaritan woman is the first recorded person
> to proclaim Jesus as Messiah to the Gentiles</u> and the
> first person to proclaim Him at all._She witnessed of
> His nature and preached to the men of her village,
> and nowhere is there any hint that Jesus criticized her
> for such actions. On the contrary, nowhere do we find
> where Jesus ever forbids a woman to preach, teach, or
> share the gospel. (Ibid, pg 35, emphasis mine)

We can be certain that the many people from her hometown who then believed in Jesus as the Messiah were profoundly thankful that she had violated any existing sexist prohibitions restricting women from teaching men:

> From that city **many of the Samaritans believed in Him because of the word of the woman who testified,** "He told me all the things that I have done." (Jn. 4:39, emphasis mine)

This passage demonstrates that God delegated teaching authority over men to the Samaritan woman in the first biblical example of Christian evangelism in all human history. The virtual celebration of this delegation in this scripture (and therefore, by God Himself, as its author) is dramatically inconsistent of God if He later planned to prohibit all future such behavior. Having so successfully accomplished the evangelization of the Samaritan town through the ministry of a woman, it is altogether unreasonable to suggest that God would later change His mind and prohibit any woman in later centuries from following her example.

In addition, there is no more profound message than what the Samaritan woman shared with her fellow townsfolk, the wonderful news contained in Jesus' Gospel of the Kingdom. If the world-changing impact of the message she relayed to her neighbors has any bearing on the matter, the fact that God chose a woman to share it should certainly certify women everywhere, in every age, to share both it and any less profound teachings to both genders in every venue. Put more simply, since God used the Samaritan woman to evangelize her entire town, that circumstance by itself completely discredits the Traditional View.

> Since God used the Samaritan woman to evangelize her entire town, that circumstance by itself completely discredits the Traditional View.

From another perspective, most scholars agree that the four gospel accounts were written many decades after Paul wrote his epistles. And the Traditional View contends that the Holy Spirit had truly prohibited women evangelists through Paul's admonitions in 1 Tim. 2:11-15. However, if the writing of that passage by Paul predates the composition of John 4:39 by several decades, then it is even more inconsistent of the Holy Spirit to include the account of the Samaritan woman's successful evangelism by Luke, much less celebrated, if the Traditional View was ever valid.

Regardless of the implications of such relative timing, it is certain that the account of her evangelism is true as recorded, and equally certain that God endorsed it, so therefore it is unjustifiably inconsistent for God, through Paul, to have subsequently prohibited the same behavior on doctrinaire grounds. Therefore, this account by itself invalidates the Traditional View.

Junia the Apostle

A woman named Junia is named as an apostle by Paul, thereby assigning to her the same spiritual office as that held by Paul himself. That recognition alone comprises proof of God's endorsement of female leaders in the Church:

Greet Andronicus and Junia, my kinsmen and my fellow prisoners, who are outstanding among the apostles, who also were in Christ before me. (Rom. 16:7, NASB 1995)

Greet Andronicus and Junia, my fellow Jews who have been in prison with me. They are outstanding among the apostles, and they were in Christ before I was. (Rom. 16:7, NIV)

Greet Andronicus and Junia, my countrymen and my fellow prisoners, who are of note among the apostles, who also were in Christ before me. (Rom. 16:7, NKJV)

For Paul to name even one woman named as an apostle is itself a demonstration of God's approval of female leadership within the Church, a circumstance which completely invalidates the Traditional View.

However, the preceding verse has been translated differently in other versions to mean that rather than naming Junia as an apostle, the apostles merely held her in high esteem:

Greet Andronicus and Junia, my kinsfolk and my fellow prisoners, who are outstanding in the view of the apostles, who also were in Christ before me. (Rom. 16:7, NASB 2020)

Greet Andronicus and Junia, my fellow Jews, who were in prison with me. They are highly respected among the apostles and became followers of Christ before I did. (Rom. 16:7, NLT)

> *Greet Andronicus and Junias, my kinsmen and [once]*
> *my fellow prisoners, who are held in high esteem in the*
> *estimation of the apostles, and who were [believers] in*
> *Christ before me. (Rom. 16:7, AMP)*

This alternate meaning is most favored by modern traditionalists, thereby supporting their assertion that there were no female apostles.

In contrast, at least three of the early Church Fathers (Origen, Jerome, and John Chrysostom) interpreted the verse to mean that Junia was an apostle on a spiritual par with Peter and Paul. These men were arguably quite familiar with ancient Greek vocabulary and usage, living as they did just a few hundred years after Paul. They also had access to original manuscripts which have now been lost to history and unavailable to modern translators. Finally, their views carry added weight given that 1,700 years of intervening cultural encroachment had not yet tainted church doctrines.

While modern scholars debate whether she was an officially recognized apostle, Junia was indisputably held in such high regard by them, and by Paul, that Paul mentioned her by name in the preceding verse. He did not so commend her because she merely provided timely and efficient housekeeping or logistical support to her male associates, or because her falafel was the best in in town. Paul here so recognized Junia precisely because she was directly participating in the public proclamation of Jesus' Gospel and did it well enough to be considered "outstanding" in that ability. Further, Paul mentions that Junia, too, was imprisoned alongside him. While substandard falafel may be considered by some to be a criminal offense, it is much more likely that Junia was imprisoned with Paul for her boldness in proclaiming the Gospel to all who would listen.

> The high view of Junia by the apostles, whether also recognized as an apostle herself or not, by itself validates the Kingdom View.

In conclusion, the question as to whether Junia was an ordained apostle is debatable. What is not debatable is the high view of Junia held by the apostles, a view virtually certain to have reflected her active participation in public ministry to both men and women. And that participation by itself, as certified by Paul's commendation of it, legitimizes the Kingdom view while simultaneously invalidating the Traditional View.

Phoebe the Deacon

Earlier in the book of Romans, a ministry partner of Paul named Phoebe was recognized as a deacon in her local congregation. This designation by itself invalidates the Traditional View because the position of a deacon held significant spiritual responsibilities. Paul's reference to Phoebe is found in the following passage:

> *I commend to you our sister Phoebe, who is a **diakonos**-servant of the church which is at Cenchrea, that you receive her in the Lord in a manner worthy of the saints, and that you help her in whatever matter she may have need of you; for she herself has also been a*

__prostatis-helper__ of many, and of myself as well. (Rom. 16:1-2, emphasis mine)

The word translated above as the English word, "servant" is the Greek noun, *diakonos* (Strong's G1249). While not among the five-fold offices of apostle, prophet, pastor, evangelist or teacher (cf. Eph. 4:11-12), the position of a deacon was one of significant spiritual leadership in the early church. A deacon in the New Testament was not merely a person who distributed food, cleared tables, and disposed of garbage, but rather held substantial spiritual authority within her local congregation. Therefore, even one woman having been named as a deacon by Paul offers strong evidence that God endorsed female leadership and authority within the Church then, and still does today.

In this particular passage, that Phoebe's role as a deacon was one of leadership is plainly demonstrated by Paul's use of the Greek word, *prostatis* (Strong's G4368) to more accurately describe her contributions. That word carries connotations of exemplary spiritual leadership at levels far above the more menial tasks of housekeeping services. In its footnote to this passage, the Passion Translation notes that his use of this word indicates that Paul regarded Phoebe as a recognized spiritual leader in her church:

> The Greek word *prostatis* means "the one who goes first," "a leading officer presiding over many," "a protecting patroness who oversees the affairs of others," "a champion defender." It is clear that Phoebe was considered a leader, a champion, a heroic woman who was most likely quite wealthy and brought blessings to

others. The term *prostatis* implies a great status (as used in classical Greek), and denotes a high position in the church. (*The Passion Translation*, Footnote 'd' to Rom. 16:2, emphasis mine)

The Passion Translation considered the above information to be credible enough to be incorporated into its translation of the verse itself. Accordingly, Paul's high regard for Phoebe's leadership role in his own life is clearly evident in the TPT's rendering of the passage:

> *Now, let me introduce to you our dear and beloved sister in the faith, Phoebe, **a shining minister of the Church in Cenchrea.** I am sending her with this letter and ask that you shower her with your hospitality when she arrives. **Embrace her with honor**, as is fitting for one who belongs to the Lord and is set apart for Him. So provide her whatever she may need, for **she's been a great leader and champion for many – I know, for she's been that to me**.*" (Rom. 16:1-2, TPT, emphases mine)

There is certainly intrinsic spiritual honor in every necessary position within a church body, from the leadership positions of apostles and teachers down to those of janitor or administrative clerk. Since all have divine purpose and serve necessary functions, they are equally virtuous in the eyes of God (cf. 1 Cor. 12:12-31). However, Paul would have reserved such a laudatory description of Phoebe as *"...a leader and a champion for many..."* for only an exemplary spiritual leader for at least the entire local congregation.

Further, in a stunning revelation that by itself completely invalidates the Traditional View, Paul not only identifies Phoebe as a leader in her church, but he also states that he had personally submitted himself to Phoebe's spiritual leadership when he said *"...for she's been that to me."* The Apostle Paul was here quite specific in his mention of Phoebe's significant role in his life. And Paul, under the inspiration of the Holy Spirit, would not have commended Phoebe for that role in this passage (Rom. 16:1-2), but then prohibited any woman, including Phoebe, from ever doing so for any other man in another epistle (e.g., 1 Tim. 2:12).

> Paul, under the inspiration of the Holy Spirit, would not have commended Phoebe for her spiritual leadership in his life in Rom.16:1-2, but contradicted himself by prohibiting any woman, including Phoebe, from ever doing so for any other man in another epistle (e.g., 1 Tim 2:12. This incongruity alone directly invalidates the traditional notion that Paul endorsed Christian sexism.

Finally, Phoebe's exemplary stature as a spiritual leader is demonstrated in Paul's choice of Phoebe to carry his epistle to the Roman church. Having written the letter while in Corinth, but electing to not travel to Rome himself, Paul chose Phoebe to hand-carry the letter on the long and perilous journey from Corinth to Rome. Paul would only have assigned such a considerable responsibility to a person holding only his highest regard and respect. The person he chose to carry the letter would have been a true partner in ministry. The chosen agent would necessarily be one capable to not just to carry a satchel on her shoulder, but far more importantly, of credibly presenting it to the Roman congregation. Paul would have assigned such a role, not to a mere housekeeper or logistical aide, but to an already established spiritual leader:

- Who had developed an apostolic degree of personal spiritual maturity, and was accustomed to ministering at that level,
- Who agreed with Paul on every major doctrinal issue,
- Who had sufficient spiritual maturity and knowledge to then present the letter, expound upon it, explain, and defend it,
- Who had previously demonstrated the necessary abilities to accomplish those tasks.

Phoebe clearly was a gifted and recognized spiritual leader, active in her local church, and recognized as such by Paul, and thereby offers a singularly insurmountable challenge to the Traditional View.

A Deacon is a Church Leader, Not Just a Table Waiter

In the context of Phoebe's status as a deacon, I was taught many years ago that the function of a deacon in the New Testament was merely that of a menial servant who waited on tables in the setting of communal meals. If true, then Phoebe's status as a deacon offers no helpful precedent for the doctrinal viability of women holding positions of true spiritual leadership and authority in the Church. However, a careful examination of the relevant passages demonstrates that a deacon in the New Testament was a recognized church leader holding much more spiritual authority than a menial servant. Therefore, Phoebe's biblical designation as a deacon does, in fact, provide a material precedent for the Kingdom View.

The basis for the view of a deacon as merely menial servant having no spiritual authority is based upon a mistaken application of the following passage:

> So the twelve summoned the congregation of the disciples and said, "It is not desirable for us to neglect the word of God in order to **diakaneo-serve** tables. Therefore, brethren, select from among you seven men of good reputation, full of the Spirit and of wisdom, whom we may put in charge of this task." (Acts 6:2-3)

In its context, the apostles here discerned that their time was better spent on matters more critical to the spiritual leadership and welfare of the Church than the menial task of cleaning tables. And the Greek verb used here by Brother Luke to describe the act of waiting on tables is, *diakaneo*, the verb form of the Greek noun, *diakonos*, the word used by Brother Paul to describe Phoebe's position in the Church in Rom. 16:1. It is this association by which my childhood teacher then inferred that Paul's description of Pheobe as a *diakonos*-servant is merely a reference to her assignment as a menial servant. If this view is correct, then Phoebe's recognition in Rom. 16:1 as a deacon offers no helpful precedent on the topic of leadership roles of women in Christian ministry.

Two observations combine to invalidate the notion that the position of a deacon held no spiritual authority in the early church. First, at least two of the seven men appointed to wait tables were men of great spiritual stature in the early church, and who ministered with great spiritual authority. For example, we know that Stephen, one of the seven men chosen to clean tables in Acts 6:3, released great signs and wonders in the grace and *dunamis*-power of God (cf. Acts 6:8). His ministry was consequently of sufficient prominence in Jerusalem that he was infamously martyred for his clearly anointed ministry (cf. Acts 6:9-7 to Acts 7:60). Later, Philip the evangelist, also one of the chosen seven, also released signs and wonders sufficient to significantly enhance his evangelistic success (cf. Acts 8:6-8). In both cases, such ministries are hardly the work of men whose only contribution to the church was cleaning tables.

Most importantly, the notion that the position of a deacon had no spiritual authority in the New Testament is invalidated by the fact that in every case in which the noun-form of the word, *diakonos*, is used in the New Testament, it universally connotes a position of spiritual authority and leadership.

> In every case in which the noun-form of the word, *diakonos*, is used in the New Testament, it universally connotes a position of spiritual authority and leadership.

For example, Jesus used *diakonos* on several occasions to refer to a leader in the church in particular, as illustrated by the following verses:

> *It is not this way among you, but whoever wishes to become great among you shall be your **diakonos**-servant. (Mt. 20:26)*

> *But the greatest among you shall be your* **diakonos**-*servant. (Mt. 23:11)*

Jesus here referred to the most prominent spiritual leaders in the Body of Christ, the apostles, as *diakonos*-servants. Therefore, it is extremely unlikely that, by the time of the account in Acts 6:2-3, the apostles had forgotten or overlooked that connotation and applied it only to the job of waiting on tables. The apostles who appointed the seven table waiters in Acts 6:2-3 certainly knew that Jesus' use of the word, *diakonos*, here referred to leaders, or they would have appointed themselves to be table waiters if only to honor Jesus' prior words in Mt. 23:11!

> The apostles who appointed the seven table waiters in Acts 6:2-3 certainly knew that Jesus' use of the word, *diakonos*, referred to spiritual leaders, or they would have appointed themselves to be table waiters if only to honor Jesus' prior words in Mt. 23:11!

In explicit confirmation of Jesus' laudatory use of *diakonos* in the preceding verses, Paul refers to Jesus Christ Himself as a *diakonos*-servant of God:

> *For I say that Christ has become a* **diakonos**-*servant to the circumcision on behalf of the truth of God to confirm the promises given to the fathers. (Rom. 15:8)*

Paul was here clearly not describing Jesus as a menial table waiter, but rather as the greatest among them by virtue of His penultimate atoning sacrifice.

Likewise, the Apostle Paul later refers to himself, as well as the Ephesian leader, Apollos, as *diakonos*-servants on several occasions:

> *What then is Apollos? And what is Paul?* **Diakonos-***servants through whom you believed, even as the Lord gave opportunity to each one. (1 Cor. 3:5)*

> *Whereof I was made a* **diakonos**-*minister according to the gift of the grace of God given unto me by the effectual working of his power. (Eph. 3:7)*

> *Of this church I was made a* **diakonos-**minister *according to the stewardship from God bestowed on me for your benefit, so that I might fully carry out the preaching of the word of God. (Col. 1:25)*

Based on the above observations, the noun form of a *diakonos*-servant is used to describe those holding positions having only the highest possible spiritual stature in the Body of Christ, including both Jesus, the apostles, and other non-apostolic leaders. Therefore, these associations unequivocally demonstrate that Phoebe's designation as a *diakonos*-servant elevates and aligns her spiritual stature to the highest possible level, one shared by Apollos, Paul, and even Jesus Himself. Specifically, Paul's recognition of Phoebe as a *diakonos*-deacon demonstrates that Paul considered her to be an officially recognized spiritual leader in her church.

In further confirmation of this higher view of the function of a deacon, Paul's qualifications for a *diakonos*-deacon, found in 1 Tim. 3:8-13, are altogether unrelated to those needed to be an efficient table waiter. This observation further emphasizes that when Paul used the noun-form of the word, *diakonos*-servant, he was referring to a leader in the church having only the highest spiritual stature and commensurate authority.

Some traditionalists will no doubt agree that the position of a deacon includes significant responsibility and spiritual authority. However, it is self-contradictory to first endorse Paul's list of the leadership qualifications of deacons in 1 Tim. 3:8-13, only to then contend that Phoebe's status as a named deacon offers no meaningful precedent on the topic of women's rights in ministry.

> It is self-contradictory to endorse Paul's list of the leadership qualifications of deacons in 1 Tim. 3:8-13, only to then contend that Phoebe's status as a named deacon is of so little importance that it offers no meaningful precedent on the topic of women's rights in ministry.

In summary, therefore, the role of *diakonos*-deacons in the New Testament churches was one of leadership holding significant responsibility, including spiritual authority over both men and women. The fact that Phoebe is identified by Paul as a *diakonos*-deacon, alongside Jesus, himself, and Apollos, certifies that she was an exemplary spiritual leader in her church having spiritual authority over both genders, and thereby offers a resounding confirmation of the Kingdom View.

The ordination and recognition of Phoebe as a dea-coness by itself comprises a resounding confirmation of the Kingdom View.

Priscilla the Teacher

In addition to Phoebe, the life and ministry of another female ministry partner of Paul named Priscilla corroborates the Kingdom View. The high opinions of Priscilla held by Luke and Paul are demonstrated by the progressive evolution of their references to her along a biblical timeline.

In her first encounter with the Apostle Paul, Luke mentions Priscilla as only a minor biographical detail, rather than as a significant ministry partner or leader. Her mention here was as a biographical accessory in the life of the person of primary focus in the passage, her husband, Aquila:

> And he found a Jew named Aquila, a native of Pontus, having recently come from Italy with his wife Priscilla, because Claudius had commanded all the Jews to leave Rome. (Acts 18:2)

Luke here refers to Priscilla only as a descriptive qualifier to the primary focus of his reference, and the first of the couple to be named, her husband, Aquila.

Just a few short years later, however, Paul reverses the order of reference to the husband and wife used by Luke, and mentions Priscilla first in referring to the couple:

> *Greet Priscilla and Aquila my helpers in Christ Jesus:*
> *who have for my life laid down their own necks: unto*
> *whom not only I give thanks, but also all the churches*
> *of the Gentiles. Likewise greet the church that is in their*
> *house. (Rom. 16:3-5)*

Paul's order of reference here is particularly revealing, given Paul's prior, secondary of Priscilla as merely a marital accessory, and his personal history as a zealous and legalistic Pharisee of the Jewish faith. That he reversed the order of his reference, and here mentions Priscilla ahead of Aquila, indicates that Priscilla had become at least as important a ministry partner as Aquila. In fact, his listing order of Priscilla ahead of Aquila would have been perceived by Aquila as a social insult if he were not sufficiently humble, being as how Aquila would have evidently been on hand when it was presented to the Romans *("...Greet Priscilla and Aquila...")*. In addition, his history as a tradition-bound Pharisee would have predisposed him from making any favorable mention of a mere woman in any regard, much less the prominence of listing her ahead of her husband in a list of ministry leaders. His listing of Priscilla before that of Aquila both overrode centuries of cultural gender bias while also revealing Paul's high opinion of her contributions in ministry.

Paul also identifies Priscilla with a ministry stature at least equal to that of her husband by referring to them both in the same phrase as *"...my helpers in Christ,"* and by his reference to the church that meets *"...in their house."* In this context, therefore, it is clear that Priscilla is not providing only housekeeping help but is an equal partner with her husband in the public proclamation of Jesus' Gospel. It is equally clear that Paul in this passage no longer viewed Priscilla as only a biographical accessory to Aquila, but as a vital co-laborer in ministry alongside Aquila and Paul.

In addition, Paul acknowledged here that both Priscilla and Aquila had risked their own lives for that of Paul, a most unlikely gesture on Priscilla's part had her contributions been only those of merely housekeeping varieties ("… *who have for my life laid down their own necks*"). That bold, Christian women such as Priscilla were active in the public proclamation of Jesus' Gospel is corroborated by Paul's recollection that as a Pharisee, he had previously sought to imprison both male and female Christians (cf. Acts 9:1-2).

Finally, in another passage, it is revealed that Priscilla explicitly assumed the role of a teacher when both she and her husband took Apollos aside and together "…*explained to him the things of God more accurately.*" (cf. Acts 18:26). This is a clear scriptural case of a woman teaching a man, and a very important and influential man at that. Apollos was a prominent leader in the church at Ephesus. Therefore, this event would comprise a direct violation of Paul's alleged prohibition against female teachers, and the Traditional View… unless that alleged prohibition is false, and Paul never held such a view.

A committed traditionalist will likely claim that since Priscilla and Aquila taught Apollos together, her role could have been subservient to that of Aquila. If so, the account therefore does not comprise an example of a woman teaching a man independent of male supervision. I discount such an interpretation because of the way Paul described their intervention. Paul was careful to say that *"...they took him aside and explained..."*, rather than *"...Aquila took him aside and explained, and with Phoebe's help...."*. The simplest and most textually faithful interpretation here is that both Priscilla and Aquila were equal partners in the teaching of Apollos, and this verse therefore does provide a scriptural example of a woman teaching a man.

Priscilla and Aquila probably acquired their advanced knowledge of *"...the things of God..."* from their extended period of personalized discipleship by the Apostle Paul himself as they manufactured tents together (cf. Acts 18:3). In that setting, both Priscilla and Aquila would therefore have had the first-hand opportunity to learn every teaching of Paul directly from Paul himself, including his views towards women in ministry. With such familiarity, and with Priscilla having the high degree of spiritual maturity recognized by Paul, it is highly unlikely that Priscilla would then violate Paul's alleged disapproval of female teachers by presuming to educate Apollo in any spiritual matters.

> Either Priscilla violated Paul's alleged prohibition against females teaching males when she taught Apollos, or 1 Tim. 2:11-15 has been misinterpreted by traditionalists, and her act of teaching Apollos by itself legitimizes the Kingdom View.

Finally, the man named Apollos was a leader in the Ephesian church who would in turn teach many others. His role there was made even more critical by virtue of that church's location on the frontier of the advancing Christian faith. For example, Ephesus, some 600 miles from Jerusalem, was sufficiently distant from that city that the twelve Ephesian disciples had not even heard of the Holy Spirit by the time they were met by Paul some twenty years after Jesus' resurrection (cf. Acts 19:2). Therefore, if Priscilla taught Apollos anything of material significance about Jesus' Gospel, the profound and far-reaching impact of teaching such a prominent male leader in such a frontier church becomes far more impactful by extension than its simple content. Therefore, Priscilla's act of teaching Apollos offers a supporting indication of God's endorsement of women teaching men in the expanding Church at-large.

Chloe, Nympha, Apphia, Lydia, and "The Chosen Lady"

In addition to Junia, Phoebe, and Priscilla, several other women held leadership roles in the New Testament. For example, it can reasonably be inferred that Chloe (cf. 1 Cor. 1:11), Nympha (cf. Col. 4:15), "the chosen lady" (cf. 1 Jn. 1:1), and Apphia (cf. Phm. 1:2) were leaders of churches meeting in their homes. While no mention is made of the gender mix of those churches, it is reasonable to assume that they each included at least the male members of their respective households, while probably including other males. Therefore, these women would have had spiritual authority over those male congregants as well.

Also, Luke commends Lydia for leading her entire household to the Lord, including, presumably, its male inhabitants. Such an act would have required her to speak to and teach men regarding the requisite spiritual matters (cf. Acts 16:14-15). Of course, such an act would have violated Paul's alleged prohibition of women teaching men, so the case of Lydia also supports the Kingdom View.

Had Paul preferred that Lydia remain silent...or Chloe, Junia, Phoebe, or Priscilla, for that matter, as the Traditional View claims, it would be contradictory for Paul to also commend them, or for Luke to even mention them, for the same behavior of which that view disapproves.

> Had Paul preferred that Lydia remain silent...or Junia, Phoebe, Priscilla, or Chloe, for that matter...as the Traditional View suggests, it would be contradictory for Paul to commend them, or for Luke to even mention them, for the same behavior of which that view disapproves.

Philip's Four Daughters

Four additional women held positions of high spiritual authority in the early church, as indicated by the four daughters of Philip the evangelist. Each of these women was herself a gifted prophetess:

> *Now this man had four virgin daughters who were prophetesses. (Acts 21:9)*

As prophetesses, the four daughters of Philip each held the spiritual office of a prophet, as the above translation indicates. Paul elsewhere states that the office of prophet is second in spiritual authority only to that of apostles (cf. 1 Cor. 12:28:"...*first of all apostles, second prophets, third teachers...* "), an authority even higher than that of pastors or teachers.

Throughout the Bible, in both Old and New Testaments, the spiritual office of a genuine prophet comprised a position of preeminent spiritual authority, an authority that extended over any to whom God might use them to prophesy. Their spiritual authority always and without exception extended over both men and women under their jurisdictions. In not a single case was the biblical office or function of a prophet restricted or limited by his or her gender. Therefore, the fact that these four women each held such an office is self-evident proof that God endorses women holding positions of spiritual authority over men.

> In not a single case was the biblical office or function of prophet restricted by his or her gender. Therefore, the fact that these four women each held the office of prophet is self-evident proof that God endorses women holding positions of spiritual authority over men.

Accordingly, there is no biblical record of a prophet serving only his or her own gender. This absence reflects the reality that the divinely-authored truth contained in an authentic prophetic declaration is in no way dependent upon the gender of the person through whom it is revealed. Any authentic prophet, whether male or female, speaks the oracles of God regardless of their gender. His or her prophecies carry God's genderless authority, guidance, counsel, and wisdom, regardless of the genders of either the prophet or the target audience of the prophecy. The issue of whether any person is a divinely ordained prophet is debatable, of course, based upon criteria other than his or her gender. However, having once been recognized as a prophet, his or her words are to be tested as potentially the words of

God Himself...with no consideration given to the gender of the prophet:

Do not quench the Spirit; do not despise prophetic utterances. But examine everything carefully; hold fast to that which is good. (1 Th. 5:19-21)

A determined critic might contend that Paul's mention of the four prophetic daughters could mean only that they were operating with that spiritual gift (cf. 1 Cor. 12: 4-10), while not having been recognized as holding the spiritual office of prophet. While possible, Paul chose to give them the title, "prophetess", so the simplest textual interpretation is that they were divinely ordained into that office and were official prophetesses. Regardless, however, whether as an office or as a spiritual gift, general prophecies by women in the Church age were foretold by Joel (cf. Joel 2:28), and later affirmed by Peter (cf. Acts 2:16-18), so their prophecies would therefore necessarily be authentically divine, and demonstrative of ordained spiritual authority over both genders in their target audiences.

In summary, the observation that Philip's daughters were authentic prophetesses whose prophecies held authority over both men and women by itself validates the Kingdom View, while simultaneously disproving the Traditional View.

Philip's daughters were authentic prophetesses whose prophecies held spiritual authority over both men and women, a circumstance which by itself validates the Kingdom View.

Tryphaena, Tryphosa, Julia, Euodia, and Syntyche

In addition to those mentioned in preceding sections, another five women are also commended in the New Testament as demonstrating spiritual leadership. Two of these are *"…Tryphaena and Tryphosa, workers in the Lord."* *(Rom. 16:12).* While the specific nature of their activities is not here revealed, it is unlikely that Paul would have made a point of mentioning them unless their work comprised significant, direct, spiritual ministries that included teaching, leading, and ministering to all comers, including men.

Paul also refers to a woman named Julia in a similarly commendable manner:

> *Greet Philologus and Julia, Nereus and his sister, and Olympas, and all the saints who are with them.* *(Rom. 16:15)*

Rick Renner has observed that a better rendering of the original Greek language for this verse would be *"…and all the saints who are under their care,"* indicating that Julia had spiritual stature as a pastor at least equal to that of the men also mentioned. (ref. *"Home Group – Women in Ministry, Jan 5, 2015,"* by Rick Renner, online Youtube video, at *https://www.youtube.com/watch?v=Ju-nxjV5jaE,* accessed on Dec. 28, 2019).

In addition, Paul refers to two women, Euodia and Syntyche, as co-laborers in the ministry, a most unlikely reference if their only contributions had been as housemaids:

> *I urge Euodia and I urge Syntyche to live in harmony
> in the Lord. Indeed, true companion, I ask you also to
> help these women who have shared my struggle in the
> cause of the gospel, together with Clement also and the
> rest of my fellow workers, whose names are in the book
> of life. (Phil. 4:2-3)*

Paul here refers to the two women as having *"...shared my
struggle in the cause of the gospel."* a most unlikely accolade
if their only struggle had been that of laundering soiled
clothing without the benefit of running water. Further, Paul
then refers to the entire group, including the two women, as
"...fellow workers..." in the cause of the Gospel. With all due
honor and respect to cooks, housekeepers, and launderers,
Paul here is most likely referring to those working alongside
him in the direct proclamation and ministry of Jesus' Gospel,
not just on the team providing his needed logistical support.

> Paul affirms the Kingdom View by the strong acco-
> lades he gives to Tryphaena, Tryphosa, Julia, Euodia,
> and Syntyche.

Eunice and Lois

The mother and grandmother of Paul's protégé, Timothy,
also demonstrated spiritual authority over men in several
ways. Identified as Eunice and Lois, their *"...sincere faith..."*
was both visible and notable enough for Paul to commend
them for it in the following exhortation:

> *For **I am mindful of the sincere faith within you**,
> which first dwelt in your grandmother Lois and your*

mother Eunice, and I am sure that it is in you as well. For this reason I remind you to kindle afresh the gift of God which is in you through the laying on of my hands. (2 Tim. 1:5-6, emphasis mine)

Paul's attribution of Timothy's strong faith to the two women indicates that they had been instrumental in Timothy's discipleship and spiritual training. Whether through parental influence or adult discipleship, Paul stated here that they, as women, were nonetheless successful in imparting their strong faith to Timothy. It would have been contradictory of Paul (and the Holy Spirit who inspired him) to have made such an attribution in the first chapter of 2 Timothy, only to then discredit that attribution in the very next chapter of the same epistle (e.g., 2 Tim. 2:12).

Secondly, the high visibility of their faith, commended here by Paul was evidently common knowledge in the Christian community of Ephesus, and is by itself evidence that its example was beneficially instructive to their entire local congregation, including its male members.

Finally, the commendation here of the strong faith of Eunice and Lois by the Holy Spirit serves every modern Christian with the strong indication that God very much approves of women assuming vital roles in the discipleship of not only their families, but also any others who might so benefit... including any men in those associations. Accordingly, their brief mention here by itself offers further evidence of God's endorsement of the Kingdom View.

Women's Words and Actions in the Bible Indicate God's Endorsement of Their Leadership

Another indication of God's endorsement of women as leaders and teachers with spiritual authority over men is His preservation of their words and actions in the Bible. We can be certain that all Scripture is beneficial for teaching and correcting both men and women (cf. 2 Tim. 3:16). Therefore, every record of words, thoughts, or actions by women in the Bible comprises women teaching men through those words and actions, and of God's divine endorsement of them doing so.

Examples of words, thoughts or actions of women recorded in the Bible, and universally used to teach both men and women, include the following:

- Miriam's song of triumph (Ex. 15:21).
- Deborah's song of victory (Jg. 5:2-31).
- The book of Ruth.
- The prayer of Hannah (1 Sm. 2:1-10).
- Musings of the Shulamite woman (Song of Solomon).
- The Magnificat of Mary the mother of Jesus (Lk. 1:46-55).
- The Queen of the South, likely the Queen of Sheba, who was wise enough to seek out Solomon for his divine wisdom (cf. Mt. 12:42).
- The widow of Zarephath, whom Jesus cited as an example of a Gentile favored by God (cf. Lk. 4:26).
- The woman who anointed Jesus' feet with her tears (cf. Lk. 7-37-50).

- Jesus' use of women as the protagonists in five parables:
  - the persistent woman before the unrighteous judge (cf. Lk. 18:1-8),
  - the woman mixing yeast into dough (cf. Mt. 13:33),
  - the ten virgins (cf. Mt. 25:1-13),
  - the woman who found the cherished coin she had lost (cf. Lk. 15:8-10),
  - the poor widow who gave everything she had to God (cf. Lk. 21:1-4).

God is wise enough to have taught every eternal truth reflected in the passages, above, without using female agents to do so. And it would be contradictory for God to impart any spiritual truth to Christians through biblical texts authored by women, or which featured female protagonists, only to then disallow other women to teach those same truths. Therefore, the mere fact that God repeatedly used women to impart biblical truth indicates His endorsement of women as spiritual teachers and leaders.

False Doctrines Used to Effectively Invalidate Credible Biblical Precedents

God's ordination and sponsorship of female leaders throughout the Bible provide significant precedents for the unrestricted operation of women in modern Christian ministry. And the considerable success of modern female Christian leaders in ministry to both genders offers compelling confirmation of God's continuing endorsement of women in every such role. This should come as no surprise, since God is immutable, and does not change (cf. Mal. 3:6,

Js. 1:17, Heb. 13:8), and Jesus' Gospel is equally eternal and unchanging (cf. Ps. 145:13, Rev. 14:6). Accordingly, such biblically justified features of Jesus' Gospel as the unrestricted empowerment of both genders by the Holy Spirit, and the unqualified liberty of women to proclaim it and minister its truths will be as equally eternal and unchanging as the larger Gospel of which they are a part.

However, if God's preferred methods changed in the decades following Jesus' resurrection, then advocates of the Traditional View could faithfully accept as true the historical presence of female leaders and teachers in the bible while simultaneously disallowing God's endorsement of female leaders and teachers in modern times. Accordingly, the following sections introduce and discredit the two most common false teachings used by traditionalists to disallow biblical precedents of women leaders and teachers, namely, dispensational cessationism and the transition view.

Dispensational Cessationism

Dispensational cessationism is a contrived, extra-biblical false belief having two component elements and is often used to support the Traditional View. As a stand-alone belief, "cessationism" is the false, anti-biblical doctrine that God stopped His release of any supernatural ministry through ordinary Christians, regardless of their gender, following the death of the last of the original twelve apostles. Regarding the main topic of this book, this false belief discounts any modern significance, for example, of the four daughters of Philip who were prophetesses: if their prophetic office and gift have ceased to function in modern

Christianity, then their example offers no meaningful precedent for modern Christians.

In concert with its first cousin of cessationism, dispensationalism is a related false doctrine that divides biblical chronology into distinct periods of time during which God relates to men in ways and processes unique to each period. The doctrine does not contend that God has changed, only that the ways in which He relates to men have changed. It also then presumes that the features of any one of these methods do not overlap each other nor extend into other times or dispensational periods of time.

Classical dispensationalism correctly notes such progressive differences in God's methods as the those between the various covenants, (e.g., Abrahamic, Mosaic, Davidic, and Jesus' New Covenant). However, the advocates of this doctrine then further subdivide the biblical timeline into increasingly smaller periods of time, or "dispensations" that have no corresponding, credible biblical justification. They will cite generalized biblical references to ages past, present, and future (e.g., Eph. 2:7-16), references which lack any mention of specific changes in how God will relate to men. Despite that lack, they then arbitrarily impose upon those references flagrantly suppositional inferences that are simply not present in the text. These contrived inferences are then used to support smaller and smaller, extra-biblical dispensations. The most egregious of such artificial segmentations is the one used by cessationists, the one that they allege separates the apostolic age in which saints released miracles from the modern church age. At the same time, they freely use the same artifice to eliminate the modern relevance of the multiple precedents in the New Testament of female prophets and Christian leaders such as Junia, Phoebe, and Priscilla.

"Dispensational cessationism," therefore, is the combination of the two false doctrines into a system that conveniently allows its advocates to selectively discount biblical precedents of any type that contradict their preferred doctrinal perspectives. Such advocates will zealously claim to be honoring the Reformation watchword of *Sola Scriptura*, while in the very act of ignoring it. For example, these advocates will resoundingly endorse Jesus' Great Commission (cf. Mt. 28:18-20) and its admonition that we are to obey all of Jesus' commands, only to then selectively disregard those of Jesus' commands that contradict their doctrine (cf. Jesus' commands to heal the sick and raise the dead, Mt. 10:7-8).

Tragically, any modern application of the supernatural ministries of Jesus and His apostles and disciples is the primary victim of these nefariously false doctrines. Its adherents universally restrict supernatural ministry in the New Testament to serving the single purpose of authenticating Jesus' message and the scriptures that record it. And having once accepted the false doctrine as true, it can also then be conveniently used to invalidate any modern application of the multiple biblical precedents of women in Christian ministry.

In the case of Christian sexism, for example, dispensational cessationism allows its advocates to fully accept God's ordination of a female judge (Deborah) in the Old Testament, and a female deacon (Phoebe), the four prophetically gifted daughters of Philip, a female apostle (Junia), and a female teacher (Priscilla) in the New Testament. However, they do so while simultaneously discounting God's modern ordination of women in such roles, since dispensational cessationism eliminates any modern impact of these precedents.

Since the biblical canon is closed, no supernatural certification of new scripture is needed, so dispensational cessationism can logically claim there is therefore no further need of any supernatural ministry. However, the supernatural ministry in the New Testament can easily be shown to fill multiple other functions that have been, and will be, essential to the successful function of Jesus' true Church for its entire history. For example, in addition to authenticating Jesus and the Bible, a partial list of these other functions include:

- To continue and perpetuate the glorification of God and Jesus (Jn. 11:4),
- To destroy the works of satan in the lives of individual Christians (1 John 3:8b),
- To serve as integral elements of the Gospel itself as it is proclaimed (1 Cor. 4:20),
- To act as a compelling catalyst and aid for evangelism (Acts 3:8-9, Acts 4:4, Rom. 15:19),
- To provide an independent basis for genuine faith of individual Christians (Jn. 10:38, 1 Cor. 2:4-5).

The overwhelmingly tragic result here is that, if supernatural ministry serves multiple purposes whose demands extend into the church age, but has not been occurring because of restrictions imposed by these false doctrines, then any such needs have been unmet, to the collective and ongoing detriment of the Church. Considering the virtual collapse of the Western Church over the last one hundred years, I propose that dispensational cessationism is among the primary causes of that collapse.

The Transition View

Another false doctrine often used to support dispensational cessationism, and the Traditional View by extension, is a perspective I characterize as the "Transition View." This view dismisses the modern doctrinal influence of any biblical precedent found in the parts of the Bible characterized by its advocates as belonging to one of several so-called "transition" periods of biblical history. Its advocates reason that during such transition periods, God's processes were in a state of change from one dispensation to the next sufficient to render them unreliable for modern doctrinal formation.

For example, the most egregious mistake of the advocates of the transition view is their contention that a dispensational "age of grace" began soon after the book of Acts was written. Accordingly, only the Epistles are fully reliable for modern doctrinal formation. Consequently, the four synoptic Gospels and the book of Acts, as well as surgically redacted portions of the epistles to the Romans, Corinthians, Ephesians, and Thessalonians, are sufficiently transitional that their influence on modern doctrine must be at least carefully sifted through the filter of the Epistles, or in specific cases denied altogether. Incredibly, the Transition View must necessarily revise "Sola Scriptura" to a more qualified version, "Sola Scriptura that agrees with my extrabiblical doctrine." In doing so, they must necessarily discount the very words of Jesus Himself, as well as the Apostle Paul.

For example, advocates of the transition view commonly accept the universal truths contained in such revered passages as Jesus' Sermon on the Mount (cf. Mt. 5:1-7:29), the Great Commission (cf. Mt. 28:18-20), and Paul's famous chapter on *agape*-love (cf. 1 Cor. 13). However, they then nimbly cite the transition view to entirely dismiss passages that contradict their cessationist views. They contend that these allegedly troublesome passages belong to a prior, now-extinct transition period, and are therefore not credible for modern doctrinal formation. In effect, they thereby allow their false, extra-biblical doctrines to redact any nonconforming scriptures. Such passages include, for example,

- commanding a figurative mountain to move in Mt. 21:21,
- doing greater *ergon*-works (miracles) in Jn. 14:12,
- receiving contemporary, individual revelation directly from the Holy Spirit in Jn. 16:13,
- Paul's repeated declarations that authentic proclamation of the Gospel must be corroborated by attendant supernatural ministry (cf. 1 Cor. 2:4-5, 1 Cor. 4:19-20, 1 Th. 1:5, Heb. 2:3-4, Rom. 15:19), and
- Paul's otherwise explicit and direct instructions regarding spiritual gifts in 1 Cor. 12 and 1 Cor. 14.

Advocates of the Transition View are constrained to either accept or dismiss biblical passages on a cycle so frequent and sudden as to expose its adherents to exegetical whiplash. Only to conform to the ponderous weight of a time scale preferred by dispensationalists, the following list is presented on a linear scale of time. The list accepts the consensus views of modern scholars, that three books were authored by Paul in the following order in time: 1 Corinthians, Romans, and 1 Thessalonians. It demonstrates at least eighteen times the Transition View must violate its own demand of inviolate dispensations by accepting or effectively rejecting well-known scriptural passages to preserve its arbitrary and unbiblical presumptions:

- Accept the Sermon on the Mount and the Beatitudes (Mt. 5-7):
- Dismiss or explain away Jesus' prophecy that Christians would do greater *ergon*-works (Jn. 14:12):
- Accept a version of the Great Commission, if only one that is limited to teaching some things of Jesus, just not all things (Mt. 28:18-20):
- Dismiss the entire book of Acts:
- Accept 1 Cor. 1 through 1 Cor. 2:3:
- Dismiss 1 Cor. 2:4-5, because it reveals Paul's outspoken reliance on miracle evangelism.:
- Accept 1 Cor. 2:6 through 1 Cor. 4:18:
- Dismiss 1 Cor. 4:19-20, because Paul therein emphasizes the importance of supernatural ministry in the ordinary life of the Church:
- Accept 1 Cor. 4:21 through 1 Cor. 11:
- Dismiss 1 Cor.12 and its revelations regarding supernatural spiritual gifts, because the Traditional View disallows any supernatural features of spiritual gifts:
- Accept 1 Cor. 13 marvelous revelations about *agape*-love:

- Dismiss 1 Cor. 14 and its revelations regarding super-natural spiritual gifts, again, because the Traditional View disallows spiritual gifts:
- Accept 1 Cor. 15 and subsequent chapters in the book:
- Accept Rom. 1:1 through Rom. 15:18:
- Dismiss Rom. 15:19 and its emphatic reference to supernatural ministry as comprising a critical part of Jesus' complete Gospel:
- Accept Rom. 15:20 to 1 Th. 1:4:
- Dismiss 1 Th. 1:5 because of its emphasis on super-natural, miracle evangelism:
- Accept 1 Th. 1:6 to 1 Th. 5:18:
- Dismiss 1 Th. 5:19-21 because of its command to accept contemporary prophecy:
- Accept the remainder of the New Testament, except any other isolated parts they must dismiss even then (e.g., 2 Tim. 3:5, Heb. 3:15).

If even one scriptural passage is thereby ignored, and without biblical justification, then an exegetical mistake of the worst sort has been made. And explaining away its clear meaning with flawed interpretation breeds the same corrupt result as ignoring it altogether. Either process comprises an effective rejection of the passage itself, whether the critic would feel comfortable with such a description. Picking and choosing which verses (and even entire books) to accept or effectively reject based on unbiblical doctrines is a sure route to dogmatism, heresy, and ultimately, dissolution... which is precisely the combination of challenges facing mainstream Christianity today. The multiple rejections reflected above, including the entire book of Acts, reflects a selection bias so flagrantly dangerous as to comprise heresy on par with the worst in history, and is certain to be the work of satan himself.

> Making an utter joke of the Reformation watchword, "Sola Scriptura," the multiple rejections reflected on the preceding list, including the entire book of Acts, reflects a selection bias so flagrantly dangerous as to comprise heresy on par with the worst in history, and is certain to be the work of satan himself.

To be clear, I celebrate every devout Christian as my brother in the family of God. However, no one is exempt from deception, and even worse, devotion to false doctrines becomes idolatry when one uses them to redact multiple biblical passages. And citing scriptures in his defense rings quite hollow if one's redactions make his Bible look like one of those "classified" documents from an intelligence file, one whose every second line is obscured with black ink.

All three mistaken beliefs (cessationism, dispensationalism, and the transition view) are easily shown to be not only entirely extra-biblical, but anti-biblical, as well. They each comprise false doctrines that have not only revised and diluted Jesus' original, complete Gospel of the Kingdom of God, but have effectively redacted significant passages and emphases altogether.

As so woefully prophesied by the Apostle Paul, the advocates of these three false beliefs are effectively holding to a form of godliness, while denying its miracle-working *dunamis*-power (cf. 2 Tim. 3:5). Their methods reveal that their underlying goal is not to honor scripture, but to discount any modern supernatural activity of God. One major side effect is their corresponding disregard for biblical precedents of female Christian leaders.

> Cessationism, dispensationalism, and the transition view, **by deliberate design**, each comprise false doctrines that have reduced Jesus' own version of His Gospel to one that is completely lacking any of its original, supernatural content.

Having already reduced the influence of mainstream Christianity in Western Europe to an all but invisible image of its former dominance, satan continues his full exploitation of these effective redactions in the USA. Tragically, all three misbeliefs, false though they are, nonetheless systemically saturate the beliefs and teachings of most mainstream Protestant sects. They are rigorously taught and promoted in their seminaries, are universally taught in their churches, and consequently are accepted by most rank-and-file members of those sects.

A thorough refutation of these three beliefs is far beyond the scope of a small section of this book. Very briefly, however, their considerable, even insurmountable, failings include the following:

- None of them possess explicit biblical support. Not a single verse in the Bible explicitly details the views promoted by cessationism, dispensationalism, or the transition view.
- Lacking any explicit biblical foundation, all three are necessarily justified solely based on extra-biblical

inference, supposition, and even church tradition. All of these are easily shown to contradict clear scriptural statements and emphases to the contrary.

- In most cases, their supporting suppositions are easily demonstrated to be wholly false. For example, the Greek word, *propheteuo*, does not mean "preaching", never has and never will. For another example, the miracles in the New Testament are easily shown to have served, and continue to serve, multiple other major purposes besides authenticating Jesus and scripture.

- Most alarmingly, all three explicitly and directly contradict multiple, plainly stated passages in the Bible, and require their advocates to effectively censor and redact central emphases of Jesus and Paul (e.g., 2 Tim 3:16, Lk. 10:19, Mk. 11:22-24, Mt. 17:20, Jn. 16:13, 1 Cor. 1:7, 1 Cor. 2:4-5, 1 Cor. 12:7-11, 1 Cor. 14:1-40, Rom. 15:19, Eph. 4:11-13, and 1 Thess. 1:5).

- In total, the weaknesses in their justifications make a mockery of the watchword of the Protestant Reformation, *Sola Scriptura* ("only scripture"). Their advocates offer a sort of superficial honor to scripture, but only until it no longer supports their doctrine.

A thorough and compelling discussion of these three false doctrines would easily fill another book, and to that end I am now writing just such a book. For readers too impatient to wait for that work, several other authors with views of this topic sympathetic to my own can be readily consulted. In that direction, I recommend the following works:

DeArteaga, William; *Quenching the Spirit*. Creation House, Lake Mary, FL, 1992,

Grieg, Gary, and Springer, Kevin; *The Kingdom and the Power*. Regal Books, Ventura, CA, 1993,

Deere, Jack; *Surprised by the Power of the Spirit*. Zondervan Publishing House, Grand Rapids, MI. 1993,

Deere, Jack; *Surprised by the Voice of God*. Zondervan Publishing House, Grand Rapids, MI. 1996.

In summary, while God has endorsed women as leaders and teachers throughout the Bible, it is only by the adoption of the anti-biblical, false doctrines of cessationism, dispensationalism, and transition that these decisively compelling precedents can be effectively ignored by traditionalists.

CHAPTER 7

God Endorses Women Leaders in the Kingdom of God

IN ADDITION TO THE women leaders and teachers specifically mentioned by name in the Bible and presented in preceding chapters, the following discussion reviews additional biblically based justifications of the Kingdom View. These include the following:

- Jesus' emancipation of women.
- Paul's confirmation: "Neither male nor female".
- There is no sexism in the Kingdom of God.
- The spiritual offices and gifts have no gender distinctions.
- Joel specifically foretold female prophets in the Church age.
- David's messianic prophecy of a great host of women.
- Peter's "royal priesthood" comprises both genders.
- The Kingdom View promotes spiritual life and liberty.
- The harvest is plentiful, but the workers are few.
- Gender bias in the Church comprises a virtual rejection of God.

- The Women's Awakening is part of God's restoration of Jesus' complete Gospel.

Jesus' Emancipation of Women

Among the most compelling justifications for gender equality in Christian ministry is Jesus' dramatic emancipation of women in His own ministry. In direct violation of the many sexist cultural restrictions of His day, Jesus showed no gender favoritism in His teaching and discipling. He chose instead to relate to every woman He encountered with the same divine love, compassion, favor, dignity, and respect with which He related to men:

- He welcomed women as ministry partners, traveling companions, and financial supporters,
- He taught, spoke, related, and ministered to women as well as men as equals, in stark contrast to every Jewish rabbi of His day,
- His parables feature both men and women as their protagonists, something any sexist proclivity on His part would have avoided.

The same Jesus who repeatedly violated other Sabbath traditions and side-stepped the existing Jewish hierarchy by ministering directly to the unwashed masses also violated multiple Jewish gender-based traditions. Most significantly, Jesus taught and ministered to both genders with equal compassion, love, and devotion. He did so to women and men alike, in direct violation of deeply set traditions which dominated such activities. In so doing, He repeatedly, persistently, and unapologetically overrode the gender bias so systemically pervasive in Jewish culture of that day. He replaced that bias with the far superior gender equality in which men and women were originally created, the same equality that so essentially characterizes the gleaming sanctity, blinding purity and untainted righteousness of the Kingdom of God. This behavior, so frequently repeated throughout His public ministry, compellingly demonstrates and justifies the Kingdom View.

Jesus, then and now, loves every person, male, and female, with a boundless and truly unconditional love that knows no limits. God is love, and Jesus is God...therefore, Jesus is love. And "everyone" includes lepers, sinners, widows, orphans, the destitute....and women. Yes, that's right... the least, the lost, the unwashed...and in a big surprise to ancient and modern cultures dominated by men...women, too! For example, it is impossible to imagine Jesus specifying the seating chart for one of His teaching sessions such that only men could occupy the front rows and seats of highest honor.

To then contend that Jesus would love and respect every other oppressed soul so unconditionally, but He would then qualify that love for women by limiting their ministry roles on the sole basis of their gender, reflects a profound lack of comprehension of the very character of *agape*-love itself. The *agape*-love of Jesus is truly unconditional, and is not dependent on the intelligence, performance, social standing.... or gender... of its human vessel or object, or to any situational, societal perception of the relative worth of that par

> Jesus related to every person as if each of them equally reflected God's own image, whether the person was Jew or Samaritan, slave or free... or male or female.... precisely because it is true. Jesus viewed each person as equal in the eyes of God....because they are.

Jesus demonstrated His high view of women in multiple ways throughout His three years of public ministry. Among His most profound demonstrations of this high view was when He equated women with men in His inaugural use of the phrase, "daughter of Abraham":

And this woman, a daughter of Abraham as she is, whom Satan has bound for eighteen long years, should she not have been released from this bond on the Sabbath day? (Lk. 16:13)

Jesus instantly eliminated multiplied centuries of gender bias when He identified the woman in this passage as *"...a daughter of Abraham..."*. In its first use in human history, this phrase would have immediately caught the attention of every Jewish scribe in Jesus' audience for its stunning implications. By using it, Jesus instantly and eternally vested women as joint heirs with men into every blessing promised to Abraham in his original covenant with God. Jesus here recognized women as co-heirs with men of the promissory covenant God made to Abraham (cf. Gen 12:1-3), completely independent of their gender. And every blessing promised to Abraham comprises all things pertaining to the Kingdom of God... necessarily including every related Kingdom function, or ministry role in that Kingdom, such as leading or teaching men.

> Jesus instantly and eternally vested women as co-heirs with men of every blessing promised to Abraham... which necessarily includes every related Kingdom function, or ministry role in that Kingdom. And teaching and leading are unequivocally included in those roles.

Only our magnificent Savior, Wonderful Counselor, God Incarnate, the Word in flesh among us, could so brilliantly establish gender equality for all time, in every venue and ministerial assignment by His marvelous application of such an otherwise simple, three-word phrase. The Kingdom of God and its marvelous aspects and features (spiritual redemption, eternal life, physical health, demonic deliverance, material prosperity) are the primary blessings promised in the Abrahamic Covenant. Therefore, when Jesus instantly vested women as equal heirs to those blessings, He thereby instantly eliminated any gender bias in that Kingdom. And this vesting necessarily applies to every ministry function that are elements of that Kingdom, certainly including leading or teaching its citizens.

> Only our magnificent Savior, Wonderful Counselor, God Incarnate, the Word in flesh among us, could so brilliantly establish gender equality for all time, in every venue and ministerial assignment by His marvelous application of such an otherwise simple, three-word phrase, "daughter of Abraham."

Jesus' gender-neutral attitudes were not merely academic in nature. He also demonstrated His total lack of gender prejudice by His egalitarian teaching methods. For example, He demonstrated these attitudes when He allowed Mary to sit at His feet and learn as He taught:

> *Now as they were traveling along, He entered a village; and a woman named Martha welcomed Him into her home. She had a sister called Mary, who was seated at the Lord's feet, listening to His word. (Lk. 10:38-39)*

In allowing Mary to sit at His feet, Jesus violated the standing Jewish religious traditions of the day. These traditions prohibited women from being taught the Torah by a rabbi in any venue. Jesus' teachings were certainly superior to those of the Torah, and He was willing to impart them without regard to the gender of His students. Jesus clearly held no aversion to teaching women...precisely because of His lack of gender bias in all spiritual matters.

In addition, Jesus routinely spoke to women in public, thereby exhibiting a dramatic departure from Jewish cultural norms of the day. For example, He spoke publicly to:

- The Samaritan woman at the well (Jn. 4:1-42),
- The woman caught in adultery (Jn. 8:1-11),
- The Syrophoenician (Canaanite) woman (Mt. 15:21-28),
- The widow of Nain (Lk. 7:11-13),
- The woman with the issue of blood (Lk. 8:43-48),
- The crippled woman bent over for eighteen years (Lk. 13:10-17).

In the Jewish culture of that time, Jewish priests, scribes, and rabbis, all males themselves, taught only all-male audiences: they were not permitted to teach women. Further, any Jewish man in good standing would have committed a major cultural offense, and degraded his own social standing, by speaking to any Jewish woman in public with whom he was not already acquainted or related. Even more egregious would have been a Jewish man speaking to any woman caught in clear violations of Jewish law, or from a cultural group considered by the Jews to be as inferior (e.g., Samaritans, other non-Jewish Canaanites, Egyptians, Greeks, etc.). And yet Jesus did all these things to the certain surprise of those women and for our continuing benefit.

In addition, Jesus showed no sexism in His public ministrations of healing and deliverance, choosing instead to minister without favoring men over women. For example, He did not make women wait at the end of the line until every man had received ministry. Rather, Jesus ministered to every person in the order in which they caught His attention. Also, on two separate occasions, He allowed unacquainted women to anoint His feet with very expensive ointments, acts that violated multiple Judaic, gender-driven standards of public conduct (cf. Lk. 7:36-50 and Mt. 26:6-13).

Jesus' lack of gender bias is also demonstrated by His use of women as the featured protagonists in four of His illustrations and parables, including the woman before the unrighteous judge (cf. Lk. 18:1-8), the woman mixing yeast into dough (cf. Mt. 13:33), the ten virgins (cf. Mt. 25:1-13), the woman who lost one of her ten silver coins (cf. Lk. 15:8-9), and the poor widow who gave her last two coins to God (cf. Lk. 21:1-4). Had Jesus embraced the sexism so pervasive within Jewish culture, He could have easily taught these lessons using male protagonists with only slight changes to their story lines. That Jesus featured women in any important way in His parables demonstrates a distinct lack of gender bias on His part.

Finally, the dual facts that Jesus chose to minister directly to individual women, and that God chose to then preserve Jesus' ministry to them for all time as featured elements of the four synoptic Gospels, offer still more demonstrations of the divine elevation of the status of women as spiritual equals with men.

In addition to their featured roles in several parables, Jesus chose to teach and minister to women, and God chose to preserve those testimonies in the Bible, precisely to demonstrate the absence of any gender bias on His part. Such ministrations include:

- The woman at the well (Jn. 4:1-42),
- The woman caught in adultery (Jn. 8:1-11),
- Peter's mother-in-law (Mt. 8:14-15),
- Dialogue with Mary and Martha over their priorities (Lk. 10:38-42),
- Dialogue with Mary and Martha over their grief (Jn. 11:1-44),
- Daughter of Jairus (Mk. 5:35-43),
- The son of the widow of Nain, raised from the dead (Lk. 7:11-17),
- Two women anoint Jesus' feet with expensive perfume (Lk. 7:36-50, Matt. 26:6-13),
- The woman with the issue of blood (Mt. 9:20-22),
- The young girl raised from the dead (Mt. 9:23-25),

- His dialogue with, and healing of the daughter of, the Syrophoenician woman (Mt. 15:21-28),
- The crippled woman bent over for eighteen years (Lk. 13:10-17).

Jesus chose to teach and minister to women, and God chose to preserve those testimonies in Scripture, for the express purpose of demonstrating the absence of any gender favoritism or preference on His part.

The featured prominence of women in these accounts, and the relative frequency and persistent presence in His ministry of such encounters, completely reversed and overrode the systemic sexism so prevalent in Jewish culture of that day. In addition, they offer hard evidence of Jesus' lack of gender bias in every aspect of His Kingdom activities. Most importantly, and essential to the success of our modern Christian lives, Jesus' behavior perfectly manifested the Kingdom behavior every Christian should strive to imitate. Accordingly, to then contend that God might condone Christian sexism in His ministry assignments within that same Kingdom would require God to be impossibly inconsistent. Finally, it would require men to be sexist when Jesus, our perfect ministry model, was not.

Based upon the preceding observations, our beloved Jesus, Word-in-flesh among us, would be surprised and probably quite disappointed to be told that traditionalists not only disagree with Him, choosing instead to impose sexist restrictions on women in ministry, but that they do so in His name.

Jesus would be surprised, and quite disappointed, to
be told that, not only do traditionalists impose gender
biases and prohibit women teachers, but they do so
in His name.

In conclusion, if Jesus demonstrated such a high view
of gender equality, then so too should every Christian,
extending to his accommodation for women as leaders, pastors, and teachers.

Paul's Confirmation: "Neither Male Nor Female"

Among the strongest confirmations of the Kingdom View
is the explicit revelation by the Apostle Paul of the absence
of gender inequalities within the ideal Body of Christ. The
following verse clearly states that the spiritual standing of
every Christian, in Christ, is identical to that of every other
Christian:

> For you are all sons of God through faith in Christ Jesus.
> For all of you who were baptized into Christ have clothed
> yourselves with Christ. There is neither Jew nor Greek,
> there is neither slave nor free man, **there is neither
> male nor female; for you are all one in Christ Jesus**.
> And if you belong to Christ, then you are Abraham's
> descendants, heirs according to promise (Gal. 3:26-29,
> emphasis mine)

Therefore, according to the Apostle Paul, women are
co-equal in their spiritual standing alongside men "in
Christ." This designation describes a single group of people
that includes those in the Kingdom of God, a state of being

whose attributes the Church should aspire to reflect. Most germane to this topic, this group has no internal gender-based distinctions. Regarding their positional spiritual status within that Kingdom, Paul's statement allows for no subservient class of Christians that has any less spiritual stature on any basis, and certainly no distinction based on sexism. According to Paul, whether sons or daughters, both *"...are all sons of God..."* and *"...descendants of Abraham..."*, all equally and jointly vested in precisely the same inheritance accruing to those entitled to Abraham's spiritual legacy.

It is highly meaningful that Paul had written the preceding passage to an active, believing group of Christians as to whether they should obey Jewish law. Paul had written the passage for the specific purpose of refuting unjustified religious bias within the church. However, in so doing, he simultaneously refuted other forms of unjustified bias, including Christian sexism.

Elsewhere, Paul reveals that every Christian has been seated in the same high position of spiritual authority as every other Christian, on the same lofty spiritual plane as the Lord Jesus Himself:

> *and raised us up with Him, and __seated us with Him__ in the heavenly places in Christ Jesus, (Eph. 2:6, emphasis mine)*

Paul's use of the gender-less word, *"us"* here carries no connotation of sexist bias. In explicit contrast to the Traditional View, however, Paul's description of *"us"* being seated with Christ in the heavenly places is a clear reference to the preeminent spiritual authority that attends that supremely elevated position. Being seated anywhere in an ancient throne room was a position of high honor, but to be seated adjacent to the reigning monarch, and at his same level, automatically conferred the sovereign's highest level of favor to those so seated. Furthermore, any seat with Christ at the right hand of God (cf. Hb. 1:3, Hb. 1:13, Eph. 1:20, Col. 3:1), confers both the approval of God and His delegation of spiritual authority to those so seated. And in that seating and its automatic assignment of spiritual authority, both men and women hold equal positions.

> In explicit contrast to the Traditional View, Paul's description of "us" being seated with Christ in the heavenly places is a clear reference to the spiritual authority that attends such a lofty position. And in that seating and its automatic assignment of spiritual authority, both men and women hold equal positions.

The adoption of the Traditional view and its sexism would automatically force its advocates to interpret Eph. 2:6 in a most awkward, extrabiblical way. The Traditional View would necessarily force Eph. 2:6 to mean that there exists at least two types of seats in heavenly places next to Jesus, those having the allegedly superior authority of men, and those having the allegedly inferior authority of women. Such a notion is scripturally unjustified, of course, posing instead a substantial interpretive contradiction for those advocating for the Traditional View.

In a similar way, Paul referred to every Christian as the generic child and fellow heir of Christ, rightfully entitled to every blessing and hardship accruing to a disciple of Jesus, regardless of his or her gender:

> The Spirit Himself testifies with our spirit that **we are** **children of God, and if children, heirs also, heirs of** **God and fellow heirs with Christ**, if indeed we suffer with Him so that we may also be glorified with Him. (Rom. 8:16-17, emphasis mine)

Paul did not state or even weakly imply that the two genders had disproportionate spiritual inheritances in the Kingdom of God...because their spiritual inheritances are identical. Every feature of spiritual inheritance given to male Christians, including glory, suffering, and, yes, spiritual authority, has likewise been equally given to female Christians. According to Paul therefore, every degree of spiritual authority bequeathed to men has been equally bequeathed to women.

While the verses above address our spiritual status in the Body of Christ, they do not address each person's functional assignments within that Body. We can be certain, for example, that there will be functional distinctions for administrative purposes to facilitate the proper operation of the Body of Christ. Some few will be assigned leadership positions as apostles, prophets, or teachers, although most will not be so assigned (cf. 1 Cor. 12:29). However, if Paul had held any reservations regarding the functional ministry roles of women based only on their gender, the tone and meaning of his comments in the three previously cited passages makes no hint of this.

Whether sons or daughters, both are the equal heirs and children of Abraham, both are the figurative "sons" of God, and both are jointly vested in every aspect of Abraham's spiritual legacy and inheritance...including spiritual authority.

There is No Sexism or Gender Bias in the Kingdom of God

Every Christian should have as his primary goal in life the pursuit of the Kingdom of God (cf. Mt. 6:33). Ideally, therefore, it should be the goal of every Christian to realize every manifestation of that Kingdom in his life on Earth, just as they manifest in Heaven, to the extent that he can contribute to that end. And if gender equality can be demonstrated to be a key element of the Kingdom of God, then it should be a key element in every expression of that Kingdom...and therefore in the life of every Christian.

As it so happens, gender equality is easily demonstrated in the Garden of Eden, the Millennial Kingdom, and Heaven. These three places comprise states of being that reflect similar aspects of the Kingdom of God we have been assigned to pursue. In fact, they are similar enough that they likely each comprise a different manifestation, in different circumstances, of the same Kingdom of God. Some of the features they have in common include:

- the perpetual, manifest presence of God,
- full, unrestricted fellowship by humans with God,
- the eternal presence of peace, love, joy, and righteousness,

- the complete absence of sin, death, evil, illness, pain or suffering,
- The complete absence of any gender distinctions regarding spiritual authority.

Since there is no other conceivable state of being for humans apart from the Kingdom of God that has these attributes, the chance is very high that all three are merely different manifestations of the same, spectacularly marvelous Kingdom of God. And since there is no gender bias in any of these three manifestations of the Kingdom of God, neither should there be any gender bias regarding spiritual authority in any Earthly manifestation of that same Kingdom.

> The gender equality of the Kingdom of God should manifest in every version of that Kingdom, including the life of every Christian.

There Was No Gender Bias in the Garden of Eden

Within the Garden of Eden, in addition to no evil, pain, suffering, or death, the Bible plainly reveals that there was no gender bias regarding spiritual authority in the status of Adam versus Eve in their jointly held dominion. Therefore, since the Kingdom of God comprises a single, eternal, and unchanging entity, since the Garden of Eden was one of its manifestations, and since there was no sexism in the Garden of Eden, there should therefore be no sexism in any Earthly manifestation of that Kingdom. Those Earthly manifestation will necessarily include that which should be the first priority of every modern Christian:

> *But seek first His kingdom and His righteousness, and*
> *all these things will be added to you. (Mt. 6:33)*

The lack of gender distinctions in the Garden of Eden is initially seen in God's very first command given simultaneously to both Adam and Eve:

> *So God created man in his own image, in the image*
> *of God created he him;* **male and female created he**
> **them**. *And God blessed them, and* **God said unto**
> **them**, *Be fruitful, and multiply, and replenish the earth,*
> *and subdue it:* **and have dominion** *over the fish of the*
> *sea, and over the fowl of the air, and over every living*
> *thing that moveth upon the earth. (Gen. 1:27-28, KJV,*
> *emphasis mine)*

This particular command of God was His very first to the race of men. It was in this declaration that God revealed the overarching purpose for man. In it, both men and women are declared to be equally created in the image of God. And He gave this command equally to both Adam and Eve: *"... and God said unto them..."* God did not first tell Adam to go and make some babies with his baby-mama subordinate named Eve. Rather, God told them together, precisely because of their spiritual equality. He gave them the joint commission to *"...be fruitful and multiply..."* as equal partners in the endeavor.

Neither was Adam given more aspects of God's image beyond those given to Eve, nor was Eve denied any aspects of God's image that were given to Adam. Adam was not given more of the abilities to supervise and manage, and neither was Eve was given more of the abilities to submit and obey. Adam was not designed by God to be a better leader than Eve, or at least there is no indication of this in the first two chapters of the book of Genesis. Both were equally created in the same, singular image of God. The universally applied image of God is reflected in every person at levels of their spirits and souls much deeper than the obvious biological differences in the two sexes. For example, God created each and every man and woman to have free will, self-awareness, a moral conscience, the capacity to love and to hate, a desire for fellowship, and with a trinitarian composition comprising a body, soul, and spirit. The image of God in which we are made has far deeper attributes than any superficial differences between us such as race, physical stature, nationality, and yes, gender.

Most critical to the main topic of this book, God here delegated dominion and authority over the things of the Earth to both Adam and Eve, as equal partners, without assigning either one of the pair any kind of supervisory dominion or authority over their partner. Within the perfection that was the Garden of Eden, this delegation was therefore applicable to all men and women. Because God specified the beneficiaries of the delegation of dominion as the third person-plural, "them," any dominion or authority given to Adam was equally given to Eve ("...and God said unto **them**... have dominion...").

> Both Adam and Eve were equally created in the same, singular image of God. And because God specified the beneficiaries of the delegation of dominion as the

plural, "them," any dominion or authority given to Adam was equally given to Eve.

Certainly, God Himself later delegated some authority to husbands to "...*rule over...*" their wives:

> To the woman He said, "I will greatly multiply your pain in childbirth, in pain you will bring forth children; yet your desire will be for your husband, and he will rule over you. (Gen. 3:16)

However, the delegation here of a husband's dominion over his wife (and only a husband over his own wife) was not a part of God's original design, but comprised a consequence resulting from the fall of man. Prior to the fall of man, Adam did not "rule" over Eve, or the curse of a husband's dominion in Gen. 3:16 would not have been a curse at all, but merely a redundant and unnecessary repetition of a preexistent state. Therefore, in the first earthly expression of the Kingdom of God, men and women held positions of equal stature regarding spiritual authority in the Garden of Eden. And if this equality was true in that expression, and the Kingdom of God is both eternal and everlasting (cf. 2 Pet. 1:11), then it will be true in every other expression of that Kingdom, including its every expression in the lives of modern Christians while they are alive on Earth.

> Prior to the fall of man, Adam did not "rule" over Eve, or the curse of a husband's dominion in Gen. 3:16 would not have been a curse at all, but merely a redundant imposition of a preexistent state.

The effects of Eve's curse applied after the couple left the Garden of Eden, not while they were still living within the Garden. Further, the curse only applied to a husband's relationship to his own wife, and not to any relationship outside of their individual marriage. God's original design as reflected in their equal authoritative stature in the Garden of Eden was that men and women would share equal authority in their lives within His Kingdom. And it is this original design that Jesus' mission on Earth was intended to restore. To claim any less is to cheapen Jesus' mission, and a virtual assertion that Jesus' mission was incomplete.

> God's original design in Eden was that men and women would share equal spiritual stature, dominion, and authority in their Kingdom lives, and it is this design that Jesus' mission on Earth was intended to restore. To claim any less comprises a virtual assertion that His mission was incomplete.

In the second chapter of the book of Genesis, and still within God's original design, God offers more details about the creation of woman (e.g., it is not good for man to be alone, man needs a "helper," and Eve was formed from one of Adam's ribs – Gen. 2:18-25). Traditional interpreters will sometimes cite this reference to Eve as a "helper" as an indication that women were created to be servants to their husbands, not equal partners. Consequently, if women were created to be servants for their husbands, the assertion is then made that God gave men superior spiritual authority over women to better manage their mutual welfare. After all, someone must be in charge!

However, the mere fact of having been created as a *"helper"* carries no literal connotation of subservience in the Old Testament. The text itself, for example, speaks only to Adam's relative loneliness, not his need for a housekeeper to cook and do his laundry:

> Then the Lord God said, "It is not good for the man to be alone; I will make him a ezer-helper suitable for him. (Gen. 2:18)

God here used the Hebrew word, *ezer* (Strong's H5828) to describe Eve's relationship to Adam. In modern English usage, designating Eve as a "helper" to Adam connotes Eve as an assistant who is answerable, accountable, and subservient to Adam. However, other authors have observed that throughout the Old Testament, the Hebrew word *ezer* uniformly connotes power, strength, and responsibility in a relationship, not accountability and subservience:

> In studying the word "helper," it is astounding to note that the whole Old Testament never once uses this word (*ezer* in Hebrew) to refer to an inferior. Instead, the word most often designates God as the helper who comes to rescue Israel. A careful study of "helper" used in the Hebrew Scriptures demonstrates that it reflects power and strength and "taking responsibilities for the wellbeing" of the helpless. If the assertion that God has set [man and woman] in a nonreversible relation is true, then one has to assert that since woman, and not the man, is designated the "helper," it is the woman who is to fulfill exclusively the role of leading,

> initiating and protecting man! (May, Joe: *Setting the Record Straight*, www.cbeinternational.org)

Attributing this connotation of responsibility and strength to Eve relative to Adam in Gen. 2:18 is corroborated by the Holy Spirit being characterized as a "Helper" to humans in the Greek New Testament (cf. Jn. 14:26, Gr. *parakletos*, Strong's G3875). This use of the word, "helper", carries a connotation similar to that in the Old Testament. Like it's Old Testament connotations, the Holy Spirit as our Helper in no way suggests that He is accountable to us, He is not subservient to us, nor is He merely an assistant on hand to help us implement our own spiritual endeavors and prerogatives. To suggest that humans have any sort of dominion or authority over the Holy Spirit simply because He provides aid and assistance to them is nonsense, of course, for the aid He provides is entirely at His own discretion.

In a purely human analogy, but one also having significant spiritual elements, the office of pastor exists to serve a group of parishioners, to "help" them in effect, and to assist their spiritual growth. However, a pastor relates to his parishioners from a position of responsibility and strength. He would be woefully dysfunctional if he were to subject himself to the authority or domination of those that he serves.

Finally, some traditionalists have suggested that since Eve was deceived by satan, that Paul gave this as the reason for his prohibition on women teachers:

> *And it was not Adam who was deceived, but the woman being deceived, fell into transgression. (1 Tim. 2:14)*

Such an interpretation is unlikely for the simple reason that, while Eve was deceived and then disobeyed God in the fog of her deception, Adam was blatantly and cognitively disobedient. Eve at least could blame her disobedience on her deception, but Adam's sin was more egregious because he flatly and expressly disobeyed God while in full awareness of his act. They both sinned, and thereby earned their expulsions from the Garden of Eden. However, to contend that Eve's sin was sufficiently worse than Adam's sin so as to reduce her spiritual dependability in leadership positions would require one to believe that negligent gullibility was a more significant disqualifier for leadership than willful, open disobedience. For me, at least, I would prefer to avoid serving under a leader with either trait!

More likely, Paul was here simply reiterating the Christian view of the creation order, and to use it to rebut any carry-over from the religion of Artemis of superior authority carried by females. His point was that the belief within Greek polytheism (that women are superior to men by virtue of their superior order in creation) is false and therefore provides no credible justification for a woman to assume domineering authority over a man (see chapters 4 and 5).

In support of this interpretation, another author has noted that Paul's primary purpose in writing the letter of 1 Timothy was to advise Timothy on the challenge of false teaching that was threatening the Church at Ephesus. Accordingly, Paul referred to Eve's deception in 1 Tim. 2:14 to illuminate the power of false teaching, not to credit the fall of man to Eve's deception:

When Paul writes that the "woman was deceived and became a transgressor," he is not claiming that the fall resulted because a woman assumed authority over a man, but that false teaching led to transgression. This brings us back to the focus on false teaching that heavily occupies the letter to I Timothy. Paul is concerned with the behavioral results of this false teaching. (Young, *1 Timothy 2:11-15*, www.cbeinternational.org)

In addition, Paul had earlier revealed that God viewed the fall of man as a single sinful act, not as two dissimilar acts, first by Eve and then by Adam:

*But the free gift is not like the transgression. **For if by the transgression of the one the many died**, much more did the grace of God and the gift by the grace of the one Man, Jesus Christ, abound to the many. (Rom. 5:15, emphasis mine)*

For a traditionalist to then separate Eve's individual sin as not only separate from that of Adam, but worse enough to have contributed more to the fall of man than Adam's sin, is a clear contradiction of Paul's statement in Rom. 5:15. On this point alone, having previously more clearly expressed his precise view in Rom. 5:15, Paul's statement in 1 Tim. 2:14 was clearly not assigning the fall of man to Eve's sin as worse than that of Adam.

There Will Be No Gender Bias in Either the Millennial Kingdom or Heaven

Multiple prophets in the Bible prophesy a future time when Jesus Christ will return to the earth in bodily form. In this time, He will establish Himself as king in Jerusalem, sitting on the throne of David (cf. Lk. 1:32–33). This kingdom is commonly referred to as the Millennial Kingdom. It will be tangibly physical in its manifestation on the Earth and will last for one-thousand years.

The presence of God will be so strong in the Millennial Kingdom that many of its key features will also reflect many key elements of the Kingdom of God. These features will include the absence of gender distinctions and the institution of marriage (cf. Mt. 22:30), and the absence of any pain, suffering, or death (cf. Rev. 21:3-4). In addition, it will be a time marked by peace and tranquility (cf. Mi. 4:2–4; Is. 32:17–18), and joy (Is. 61:7, 10). Accordingly, there will be an abundance of obedience to God (cf. Jer. 31:33), Christian holiness (cf. Is. 35:8), absolute truth (cf. Is. 65:16), and the genuine knowledge of God (cf. Is. 11:9; Hk. 2:14).

The absence of gender distinctions in the Millennial Kingdom is suggested by the following verse:

> For in the resurrection they neither marry, nor are given in marriage, but are as the angels of God in heaven. (Mt. 22:30)

While this verse mentions only that the institution of marriage will be absent after their resurrection, it is reasonable to infer that any remaining gender distinctions in their resurrected bodies will either be absent altogether, or at least will play no significant role in their existence in that Kingdom. This absence will begin after their resurrection, and will then continue throughout the Millennial Kingdom and for all eternity thereafter in Heaven.

Regarding Heaven as the final manifestation of the Kingdom of God, only our spirits will translate to that wonderful place, where our spirits will no longer be tied to gender. Those parts of our beings that define our genders, our bodies and souls, will not survive the transition through death. After death we will assume our eternal, heavenly states as wholly spiritual beings. Therefore, there will be no gender identities in Heaven by which gender biases would be needed or imposed.

The Spiritual Offices and Spiritual Gifts Incorporate No Gender Distinctions

The five-fold offices of apostle, prophet, pastor, evangelist, and teacher (cf. Eph. 4:11-13) and all of the spiritual gifts (cf. 1 Cor. 12 and Rom. 12) were presented by Paul without any gender distinctions, either stated or implied. To impose such biases is textually unwarranted. This lack of bias applies both to the gender of the person who is given such an office or gift, as well as the genders of those receiving their ministries. Consequently, if God gives to a woman the spiritual gift of teaching, but she is denied the opportunity to release that gift, then God's will in the matter will have been thwarted...by the very people who were its intended beneficiaries.

> To deny the operation of any spiritual gift given to a
> woman, only because she is a woman, is to disobey the
> God who gave her the gift.

Further, spiritual gifts are given *"...for the common good..."*
(cf. 1 Cor. 12:7). If a gift of teaching, wisdom, or prophecy is
given to any single person, for example, that gift is for the
common benefit of both men and women, not just for those
of the same gender as the teacher. And God promised all
the spiritual gifts and offices, including pastoring, leadership, teaching and administration, to both men and women.

To further emphasize this concept, the Holy Spirit clearly
states in the New Testament that spiritual offices of both
genders will be given to the church for the express purpose
of equipping the saints in service, in encouragement, in faith,
and in spiritual knowledge:

> *And He gave some as apostles, and some as prophets, and
> some as evangelists, and some as pastors and teachers,
> **<u>for the equipping of the saints</u>** for the work of ser-
> vice, to the building up of the body of Christ; until we
> all attain to the unity of the faith, and of the knowledge
> of the Son of God, to a mature man, to the measure of
> the stature that belongs to the fullness of Christ. (Eph.
> 4:11-13, emphasis mine)*

Equipping the saints in the knowledge of the Son of God is
an abbreviated way of saying that designated apostles will
be leading and directing, prophets will be prophesying, pastors will be pastoring, and teachers will be teaching. And
their students will be the saints...all of them, comprising

both genders. Therefore, if God chooses a woman to be an apostle, prophet, pastor, or teacher, then this verse thereby authorizes her to fulfill that function...regardless of her gender, or the gender mix of her designated audiences. Her ordination as a teacher, for example, is by God, not man, and it is therefore God alone who chooses the people teaching His congregations.

The lack of any mention of a gender bias could be viewed as an argument from silence, except that such a lack is later expressly illustrated by the Apostle Paul himself. Paul confirmed gender equality in the spiritual offices and gifts when he explicitly allowed women to both pray and prophesy over entire congregations, in public settings, for the benefit of all those present:

> But **every woman** who has her head uncovered **while praying or prophesying** disgraces her head, for she is one and the same as the woman whose head is shaved. (1 Cor. 11:5, emphasis mine)

Paul here clearly expected women to both pray and to exercise the spiritual gift of prophecy, and to do so in public settings, as indicated by his reference to "...*every woman... while praying or prophesying...*" A determined traditionalist might contend that Paul meant for this verse to apply only to women praying or prophesying over other women, but such a contention is unjustified by this text, and is therefore purely conjectural.

Several other admonitions by Paul, by their lack of any gender-based qualifications, strongly imply that no gender qualifications are valid:

> *Pursue love, yet desire earnestly spiritual gifts, **but especially that you may prophesy**. For one who speaks in a tongue does not speak to men but to God; for no one understands, but in his spirit he speaks mysteries. But **one who prophesies speaks to men for edification and exhortation and consolation.** One who speaks in a tongue edifies himself; **but one who prophesies edifies the church.** (1 Cor. 14:1-4, emphasis mine)*

> **Let two or three prophets speak**, *and let the others pass judgment. (1 Cor. 14:29, emphasis mine)*

> *For **you can all prophesy** one by one, so that all may learn and all may be exhorted. (1 Cor. 14:31, emphasis mine)*

When Paul wrote, *"...for you can all prophesy...",* above, he offered no gender qualifiers. The word *"all"* used in the above passages is inclusive: by using it, Paul automatically included both men and women. Further, he had opened the passage in v. 14:1 by encouraging his readers to *"...desire earnestly spiritual gifts..."* with no hint of a gender bias in who could seek which gifts, a lack which is validated by his use of the word "all" in v. 14:31. Paul clearly expected here that *"all"* of those led to release any spiritual gift in a public meeting. whether it be praying, prophesying...or teaching... would be allowed to do so without respect to their gender.

> Paul clearly expected women to both pray and to exercise the spiritual gift of prophecy, and to do so in public meetings.

Public prayers do not necessarily comprise the imposition of spiritual authority by the person praying. However, the release of a prophecy is the act of speaking the oracles of God. And this entire passage was about all spiritual gifts, not just prophesying. If a prophecy is authentically divine, then it is released under divine endorsement, anointing and inspiration, and thereby comprises the imposition of divinely sanctioned authority over the intended audience. The gender of the agent delivering a prophesy is irrelevant to its authority, content, or applicability. Therefore, when Paul authorized women to prophesy in public meetings in the preceding passages, he automatically authorized women to exercise the spiritual authority of a prophet over men.

> When Paul authorized women to prophesy in public meetings in 1 Cor. 14, he thereby authorized women to exercise the spiritual authority of a prophet over men.

Based on the preceding passages, unless one contends that Paul was therein addressing only men, it would be irrational for Paul to here exhort both men and women to publicly prophesy to edify the entire church, but to then prohibit them from doing so in 1 Tim. 2:12.

You Foolish Galatians

In yet another confirmation of the Kingdom view, traditionalists must effectively deny the essential work of the

Holy Spirit in empowering a Christian to minister to any successful degree. They do so when they contend that only males are adequately equipped in their soul-based temperaments to lead or teach other males, in direct denial of the essential empowerment that is only and equally available to both genders by the indwelling Holy Spirit. It is only through the empowerment of the Holy Spirit via His cohabitation with their human spirits, and the supernatural indwelling of Jesus Christ, that any Christian accomplishes any eternally beneficial ministry:

> *You foolish Galatians.... are you so foolish? Having begun by the Spirit, are you now being perfected by the flesh? (Gal. 3:1a, Gal. 3:3)*

> *I am the vine, you are the branches; he who abides in Me and I in him, he bears much fruit, for apart from Me you can do nothing. (Jn. 15:5)*

Another author has also made this same point:

> As a result of the Spirit's work, God's reign is open to all flesh—men and women of all ages, races, and classes. We do not earn salvation, nor does salvation depend on our sexual identity; we are saved by grace. Likewise, we do not carry out the work of Christ in our own strength, whether male or female, but in the power of the Holy Spirit. We are in error if we think that we are initiated into God's kingdom by the Spirit and then accomplish God's work by the flesh. The Spirit calls and empowers us all, and the same Spirit that dwells in women dwells in men, for there is only one

Spirit. (May, Joe: *Setting the Record Straight*, www. cbeinternational.org)

Traditionalists, of course, are unlikely to contend that the quite singular Holy Spirit somehow empowers men to teach to a superior degree over that of women. To do so would reflect a profound, and unjustifiably inflated, misunderstanding of their own role in the process, for the Bible nowhere reveals such a gender-based distinction.

Traditionalists may then argue, in the absence of direct scriptural support, that the Holy Spirit simply chooses to more powerfully empower men than women in His inscrutable sovereignty to honor the superior authority they claim God has given to all men. While such a perspective is possible, it is only conjecture since it lacks any credible biblical support (see chapters 4 and 5).

Joel Specifically Foretold Female Prophets

In still another scriptural demonstration of the Kingdom view, the authentic operation of female prophets in the Church during the church age was both foretold by the prophet Joel, and then specifically confirmed by the Apostle Peter:

> *And it shall come to pass afterward that I will pour out my Spirit **on all flesh; your sons and your daughters shall prophesy**, your old men shall dream dreams, your young men shall see visions. (Joel 2:28, emphases mine)*

> *But this is what was spoken of through the prophet Joel:*
> *And it shall be in the last days, God says, that I will pour*
> *forth of My Spirit __on all mankind__; and __your sons and__*
> *__your daughters__ shall prophesy, and your young men*
> *shall see visions, and your old men shall dream dreams;*
> *even on my bondslaves, __both men and women__, I will*
> *in those days pour forth of My Spirit, and they shall*
> *prophesy. (Acts 2:16-18, emphases mine)*

Joel first said, *"...all flesh...",* that Peter later restated as *"... all mankind..."* both of which plainly include both males and females. However, in a divinely explicit invalidation of the Traditional View, Joel removed any doubt of the Kingdom nature of his prophecy by explicitly specifying that both males and females (eg., *"...sons and daughters...")* would prophesy. Peter then reaffirms the prophecy by citing it in his well know sermon in Acts 2 *("...both men and women... shall prophesy...").* The Holy Spirit here anticipated the modern need to refute the Traditional View, because He so clearly specified through both Joel and Peter that both men and women would prophesy throughout the church age.

In addition, for the Traditional View to be accurate, it must require that Paul's statements in 1 Cor. 14:34-35 *("...women are not permitted to speak...")* and 1 Tim. 2:11-14 *("...a woman must be silent...")* somehow abrogated or superseded Joel's prophecy and Peter's later citation of it. Either Joel and Peter were accurate, or the Traditional View is accurate...but one precludes the other: the statements in these passages contradict each other, are mutually exclusive and cannot both be true.

In truth, Joel's prophecy is accurate, as are Paul's statements...but the Traditional View is at fault, because it incorrectly interprets Paul's statements (see Chapters 4 and 5), and thereby creates their mistakenly imposed conflict with Joel's prophecy and with Peter's citation of it.

> Either Joel's prophecy is accurate, or the Traditional View is accurate...but one precludes the other: they are mutually exclusive and cannot both be true. Of course, Joel's prophecy is true, as are Paul's statements...but the Traditional View incorrectly interprets Paul's statements, and thereby creates their mistakenly imposed conflict with the Prophet Joel and the Apostle Peter.

David's Messianic Prophecy of a Great Host of Women

The general and very public proclamation of Jesus' Gospel by large numbers of women during the church age was also foretold by King David in the following messianic prophecy:

> *The Lord gives the command;* **_the women who proclaim the good tidings are a great host_**. *(Ps. 68:11, NASB, emphasis mine)*

> *The Lord announces the word, and* **_the women who proclaim it are a mighty throng_**: *(Ps. 68:11, NIV, emphasis mine)*

According to David here, a *"great host"* comprising a *"mighty throng"* of female evangelists will be proclaiming the *"good tidings"* of Jesus' Gospel of the Kingdom during the Church age…and hallelujah and amen to that! There is no indication in the preceding verse that their proclamations will be restricted to audiences containing only women. The most reasonable interpretation of this verse is that its mighty throng of women will be proclaiming Jesus' Gospel to both men and women, thereby prophesying that women will be teaching men, and doing so in large numbers. The Traditional View is therefore untenable, because it must impose gender restrictions on this great host of women proclaiming the Gospel, restrictions that are not present in the text of the verse.

Both Jesus and Paul Told Both Men and Women to Teach

Jesus gave the Great Commission equally to both men and women, without imposing any gender restrictions on their obedience to it:

> And Jesus came and spoke to them, saying, 'All authority has been given to Me in heaven and on earth. Go therefore and make disciples of all the nations, baptizing them in the name of the Father and of the Son and of the Holy Spirit, **_teaching them to observe all things that I have commanded you_**; and lo, I am with you always, even to the end of the age.' (Mt. 28:18-20, emphasis mine)

Every sect and denomination in every century have understood Jesus here to be commanding every Christian, regardless of gender, to follow all of His commands. It is called the Great Commission for just that reason. And teaching all Christians to obey "…all things that I have commanded you…" is deliberately inclusive and makes no exceptions for artificially imposed, man-made traditions such as either ces-sationism or gender bias. For example, all Christians, both men and women, are to *"...heal the sick, raise the dead, cleanse the lepers, cast out demons. Freely you received, freely give."* (cf. Mt. 10:8). So, too, are all Christians, both men and women, to share His Gospel and, by extension, to teach or exercise spiritual authority, as needed, over every person and audi-ence that will receive them. The Great Commission, as pro-foundly important as it is, is entirely silent regarding gender bias in the Church. Had Jesus intended for the female half of the general population to teach and disciple only women, He would have made that qualification in this seminal passage...but He did not. Therefore, Jesus here was com-manding both male and female Christians to heal, deliver, share, teach, and disciple all comers...both men and women.

Elsewhere, Paul reaffirms Jesus' Great Commission when he commands Christians to admonish and teach one another, and he does so while imposing no gender-based qualifiers:

> *Let the word of Christ richly dwell within you, with all wisdom **teaching and admonishing one another** with psalms and hymns and spiritual songs, singing with thankfulness in your hearts to God (Col. 3:16, emphasis mine)*

A determined traditional Christian, in a misguided attempt to squeeze the entire Bible through his artificial distortion of 1 Tim. 2:12, might suggest that what Paul really meant to say here was, "teach and admonish each other, but just be careful to never permit women to teach or admonish men." However, the verse itself (Col. 3:16, above) makes no such gender distinctions. Therefore, its clear meaning, in full reflection of the Great Commission, exhorts both male and female Christians to teach, admonish, and encourage all comers…both men and women.

Peter's "Royal Priesthood" Comprises Both Genders

Like Jesus and Paul, Peter also incorporated no gender bias in his views on the true spiritual identity of every Christian. For example, Peter described every member of the Body of Christ as belonging to a single royal priesthood, regardless of their gender:

> ___You also, as living stones___, *are being built up as a spiritual house **for a holy priesthood**, to offer up spiritual sacrifices acceptable to God through Jesus Christ. (1 Pet. 2:5, emphases mine)*

> *But you are a chosen race, **A royal priesthood**, a holy nation, **a people for God's own possession**, so that you may **proclaim the excellencies of Him** who has called you out of darkness into His marvelous light. (1 Pet. 2:9, emphases mine)*

In these two passages, Peter considered every believer to be a royal and holy priest. The contention that the males among those royal priests have a rank superior in spiritual authority to female priests in the same holy order, and thereby are more suitable for the jobs of teaching, leadership, and service, on the sole basis of their gender, cannot be justified by these texts. Further, Paul anticipated that every authentic believer, regardless of their gender, would eagerly *"…offer up spiritual sacrifices to God through Jesus...*", and would "*... proclaim the excellencies of Him...*" and would do so in his or her role as a holy priest in the service of Father God. Peter made no mention here of an effective system of rank or caste within this holy order of priests, one based only on gender. Peter made no mention of a system in which males monopolize every role of leadership, teaching, and authority, while female priests were relegated to subservient or secondary roles.

According to the second verse cited above (1 Pet. 2:9), both men and women have been ordained by God to "*...proclaim the excellencies of Him...*" while it imposes no gender-based restrictions on that proclamation. Thank God Almighty that Beth Moore, Marilyn Hickey, and thousands of their female spiritual kin continue to proclaim His excellencies, to every audience willing to listen, despite traditional preferences that they stay at home.

> All Christians, both men and women, are to proclaim
> His excellencies, and to every audience who will listen!

The Kingdom View Promotes Spiritual Life and Liberty

The preceding discussions have focused on scriptural proofs for the Kingdom View. A more inferential test of this issue, but one that is equally valid from a biblical perspective, can be made by comparing the types of spiritual fruit produced by the Traditional View versus the Kingdom View.

We know that spiritual liberty accompanies the Spirit of God:

*Now the Lord is the Spirit, and **where the Spirit of the Lord is, there is liberty**. (2 Cor. 3:17, emphasis mine)*

Further, we know that Pharisaical legalism is quite able to choke the spiritual, God-given *zoe*-life from otherwise authentic and vital biblical passages:

*He has made us competent as ministers of a new covenant—not of the letter but of the Spirit; **for the letter kills,** but the Spirit gives life. (2 Cor. 3:6, emphasis mine)*

Indeed, Jesus, too, had some very stern comments regarding spiritual fruit:

You will know them by their fruits. Grapes are not gathered from thorn bushes nor figs from thistles, are they? So every good tree bears good fruit, but the bad tree bears bad fruit. A good tree cannot produce bad fruit, nor can a bad tree produce good fruit. Every tree that does not bear good fruit is cut down and thrown into the fire. So then, you will know them by their fruits. (Mt. 7:15-20)

No sincerely authentic Christian would intentionally choose to walk in Pharisaical legalism and choose to bear the bad fruit of consciously restricting, quenching, or somehow disabling the liberating activity of the Spirit of God. Accordingly, the following questions can be used to compare the Traditional versus the Kingdom Views:

- Which view effectively silences fully half of the Body of Christ by imposing anti-biblical restraints on their ministries, denies to them opportunities to release their God-given spiritual gifts and anointing, forces them to disobey God's distinct commands to teach, proclaim, pray, and prophesy, denies the entire body from receiving those God-given gifts and anointing intended by God for them to have, and thereby thwarts the plainly stated intentions of God to minister to His Church through those ministries?

Answer: Traditional View.

- Which view expressly liberates those same female voices to proclaim the complete Gospel of Jesus Christ to all audiences, in fulfillment of scriptural prophecy, in direct obedience to Jesus' commands, and in full expression of their God-given gifts and anointing, thereby enabling the entire body to receive the ministry of God Himself through those God-given gifts and anointings?

Answer: Kingdom View.

- Based on those answers, which view produces spiritual liberty and *zoe*-life (cf. Jn. 10:10) within the Body of Christ, and which view suppresses or eliminates both liberty and *zoe*-life?

Answer: the Traditional View suppresses and even eliminates spiritual liberty and *zoe*-life, while the Kingdom View fosters spiritual liberty and the *zoe*-life promised to us by Jesus (cf. Jn. 10:10).

From this perspective, therefore, the Kingdom View is, far and away, the superior perspective relative to the biblical standards of obedience, spiritual liberty, and authentic *zoe*-life.

Living Under Any Part of the Law Obligates its Advocates to Obey the Entire Law

The Traditional View, by advocating that Christian sexism is normative Christian behavior, could very well be obligating its adherents to keep the entire Law of Moses in the same way that requiring obedience to any other Mosaic law would do. And the Apostle Paul was unequivocal on the negative impact of such enslaving doctrine:

> ***It was for freedom that Christ set us free; therefore keep standing firm and do not be subject again to a yoke of slavery.*** *Behold I, Paul, say to you that if you receive circumcision, Christ will be of no benefit to you. And I testify again to every man who receives circumcision, that he is under obligation to keep the whole Law. You have been severed from Christ, you who are seeking to be justified by law; you have fallen from grace. For we through the Spirit, by faith, are waiting for the hope of righteousness. For in Christ Jesus neither circumcision nor uncircumcision means anything, but faith working through love. (Gal. 5:1-6, emphasis mine)*

In the passage, above, one could easily substitute any number of other requirements of the Mosaic Law (e.g., making blood sacrifices, eating only kosher food, observing sabbath rules, etc.) for circumcision, and thereby create the same obligation to obey the entire law. Likewise, one could also substitute the phrase, "gender bias," for each occurrence of "circumcision" in the preceding passage and still honor the core meaning of Paul's exhortation in this passage. As noted in the prior section, Jesus came to liberate us from various bondages, not obligate us to continue living under their oppressive requirements. Just ask any modern female minister of the Gospel, at least those releasing genuine spiritual fruit, whether gender bias is an effective "... *yoke of slavery...*" upon her ministry, and her answer will enthusiastically affirm this point.

The Harvest is Plentiful, But the Workers are Few

While God often does more with less, the Church should strive to use every willing worker in every available ministry position. It is misguided and even counterproductive for the Church to instead restrict the female half of its workers to only gender-specific roles.

Jesus told us that while the harvest of souls is plentiful, the number of workers willing to work that harvest are few in number:

> He told them, "The harvest is plentiful, but the workers are few. Ask the Lord of the harvest, therefore, to send out workers into his harvest field." (Lk. 10:2)

Given this circumstance, it is at least unwise and short-sighted, if not woefully counterproductive, to first ask God for more workers, but to then approve only the males among them, and to send home any females…on the sole basis of their gender.

The Example of Gladys Aylward

For a dramatic illustration of several of the preceding sections, the British missionary, Gladys Aylward (1902-1970) quite fruitfully fulfilled God's call to the mission field in China. And she did so despite formidable, institutionalized sexism, both in the Christian organizations in her home country as well as secular influences in China. And there is no doubt that had Aylward been dissuaded or prevented from implementing her ministry due to such sexism, many thousands of people would not have become Christians, hundreds of orphans would have died of starvation, while thousands of other people would have suffered horrible, life-long injury and disfigurement along with excruciating, life-long physical pain.

Thank God for Gladys Aylward, and her preferential obedience to the call of God over the denial of her culture.

While personally certain of her divine call to the mission field, the obstacles facing Aylward's initial deployment to China would have seemed insurmountable any but the most resolute:

- She had been rejected by every missionary society to which she applied for endorsement and sponsorship due to her lack of formal qualifications, formal education, and her status as a single, unmarried female,

- She had no personal resources or money with which to finance her missions work, except for having just enough money for a one-way train ticket to China,
- She had no supporting network in China, and had only one vague and indistinct ministry contact,
- She had no knowledge of any Asian language, Chinese or otherwise,
- She was a single, unmarried woman whose home culture profoundly oppressed the female gender in every secular and spiritual arena,
- The prevalent cultures and governments in China were at least as sexist as those of Great Britain, and therefore antagonistically resistant to a single female missionary of another race and nationality.

Despite those seemingly insurmountable obstacles, Ms. Aylward nonetheless obeyed her call by God and traveled to China in 1932, alone, unsponsored, and unsupported. She had agreed via correspondence to travel to the inland city of Yangchen, Shansi Province, to assist another self-appointed Western missionary, Ms. Jeannie Lawson. Lawson died a mere five months after Aylward's arrival in Yangchen, after which Aylward continued her work as the only Western missionary in the city. From that rather fitful start, she then went on to become one of the most celebrated Christian missionaries of the 20th century.

Initially working through the vocation of an innkeeper, Aylward's ministry comprised both classical Christian evangelism as well as social justice and benevolence. In addition to evangelizing those who stayed in their inn, her ministry opened and ran an orphanage in Yangchen, ministered to homeless and poverty-stricken families, and to inmates of the local prison. Displaced by World War II, Aylward thereafter started churches and established a home for lepers near the city of Sian. Displaced again by the Communist Chinese, she later opened another orphanage in Taiwan in 1948 that she oversaw until her death in 1970.

Regarding foot-binding, the Chinese sexism of that day was horribly reflected in this painful process. Within the upper and middle classes of Chinese society, and for purely cosmetic effect, the arches of both feet of a young woman were first broken. The smaller toes were then rolled underneath the foot and bound so tightly, continually, and for so many years, that the feet were permanently and painfully deformed. The act of walking on such deformed feet was reduced to very short steps, a behavior thought to be attractive. Tragically, it was excruciatingly painful as well.

Estimates for the total number of Chinese women subjected to this practice during the early 19th century range as high as 50 percent of the female population of the country. The fact that this wholly cosmetic procedure resulted in permanent and lifelong disfigurement, disability and excruciating pain for its victims catalyzed Aylward's opposition to it. Her outspoken opposition to this horrible practice grew to become a significant part of her ministry in China, including her designation by the government of China as an official "foot inspector."

Had Aylward trusted only in the *"...way which seems right to a man..." (Pr. 14:12)* and stayed at home (as the sexist cultures of Britain and China would have preferred), the death prophesied by that verse would have been multiplied many times over:

- Thousands of people in the region of Yangchen, Sian, and Taiwan would never have become Christians,
- Thousands of young women would have been physically and painfully disabled for the rest of their lives through the practice of foot-binding,
- Hundreds of orphans would have been condemned to horrible lives of misery, hunger, pain, and death by starvation and malnutrition.

In addition, only Heaven knows how many Christians in the modern underground House Church movement in China can trace their spiritual lineage to Aylward's missionary work.

Perhaps a male missionary could have implemented Aylward's work in her place, and with equivalent spiritual prosperity: after all, it is the Holy Spirit who does the work, if it is authentic. However, God called Aylward, she heard and obeyed despite heavy sexist resistance, God clearly endorsed and supported her efforts, and the Kingdom of God reaped the bountiful harvest of her work. Accordingly, while her work comprised a clear violation of the Traditional View, there is no doubt that God and all His angels in Heaven are celebrating her life and its considerable spiritual fruit.

Christian Sexism Comprises a Virtual Rejection of God

To impose Christian sexism or denial of any God-given spiritual gift, talent, or ability on the sole basis of gender reflects a profoundly shortsighted misunderstanding of the divine provenance of every such gift. As such, it comprises a virtual rejection of the God who authored and delegated those endowments. For example, we already know that spiritual gifts are given sovereignly by God, via the Holy Spirit, at His sole discretion:

> *But one and the same Spirit works all these things, distributing to each one individually just as He wills. (1 Cor. 12:11)*

Specifically, the gift of prophecy, and therefore the content of every authentic prophesy, is given to a prophet by God for God's own divine purposes. Any human denial of that gift or content, regardless of the gender of His chosen messenger, comprises to a rejection of its divine origin.... and thereby a rejection of Father God who bestowed it. Therefore, to reject a prophecy, a gift of teaching, or a leadership ability given to a woman by God, only because she is a female, is a virtual rejection of God Himself.

> To reject a prophecy, a gift of teaching, or a leadership ability given to a woman by God, only because she is a female, not only reflects a gross misunderstanding of the divine provenance of such a gift, but also comprises a virtual rejection of God Himself.

Further, if a teaching is authentically divine in its content, then it is true....regardless of the gender of the person through whom it is delivered. Any denial of such teaching on the sole basis of the gender of its human conduit is a direct repudiation of its essentially divine veracity. God's truth is either genuine and authentic, or not. And the gender of its human vessel simply has no bearing on its veracity.

In addition, God gives these gifts to individuals, not to edify or exalt those individuals, or so they can gain the acclamation of those to whom they minister, but to edify the Body of Christ:

> But to each one is given the manifestation of the Spirit for the common good. (1 Cor. 12:7)

To reject an authentic spiritual gift of teaching, given by God on the sole basis of an extra-biblical gender bias is not only a rejection of the God who authored the teaching, and a rejection of the divine benefit it contains. It also comprises a denial of the underlying function of the spiritual gift itself... to edify the larger Body of Christ. In fact, the Apostle Paul so clearly understood both the origin and purpose of authentic spiritual gifts, and so clearly anticipated objections such as the Traditional View, that he offered no footnote or gender-based qualifier to his related command in his epistle to the church at Thessalonica:

> Do not quench the Spirit; do not despise prophetic utterances. But examine everything carefully; hold fast to that which is good. (1 Th. 5:19-20)

Paul here simply said, "...*examine everything carefully...*" the strong implication being that those prophetic revelations from women were to be examined as carefully as any delivered through men. He certainly had this same thought in mind when he gave his expectation on women prophesying in public meetings (cf. 1 Cor. 11:5).

In addition, any gender bias towards female ministry leaders comprises a profound misunderstanding of the supernatural ability of the Holy Spirit to lead and guide every Christian. We know, for example, that every Christian, without regard to their individual gender, is explicitly told to not only listen to God's voice but to obey that voice (Ex. 15:26, Deut. 13:4, Deut. 15:5, Deut. 26:17, Jer. 7:23, Ps. 95:7-8, John 5:25, John 10:27, Heb. 3:15, Rev. 3:20). We also know that every Christian (again, without regard to their gender) is to be filled, guided, taught, helped, led, empowered and perfected by the Holy Spirit (Rom. 8:11-14, Eph. 5:18, Gal. 5:16, John 3:16, John 10:27, John 14:26, Luke 24:49, Gal. 3:3, Jer. 33:3).

Nowhere in the preceding twenty-one passages, or anywhere else in the Bible, does God qualify the quality or authority of His voice or His guidance with the overprint of a gender bias regarding His chosen human conduit. Nowhere does He either state or imply that His revelations and guidance to females will be of a lower quality, authority, or veracity than those He gives to males. Nowhere does He either state or imply that His chosen communication to a female Christian is of any less importance or applicability than one given to a male Christian. And if any teaching, spiritual gift, guidance, or ability originates in God, every authentic Christian should eagerly embrace it as the act of *agape*-love and *dunamis*-power from our loving Creator that it represents, and should in no case reject it due to Christian sexism.

> Nowhere in the Bible does God qualify the quality or authority of His voice or His guidance, or the acceptable gender of its intended audience, with the overprint of a gender bias.

In short, the quality and authority of the guidance, leadership and anointing of the Holy Spirit is devoid of gender favoritism. This is true because, in the eyes of God, there are no gender distinctions within the Kingdom of God. Any Christian female has the same God-given potential to hear and respond to the Holy Spirit as has any male. To reject the leadership, teaching, or other ministry of a female on the sole basis of her gender exposes at least a profound misunderstanding of both the divine origin of such gifting and the purpose for being given, or at worst, a completely unjustified prejudice and sexist bias.

The Women's Awakening is Part of God's Restoration of Jesus' Complete Gospel

At its most fundamental level, the Women's Awakening comprises a vital component of Jesus' complete Gospel of the Kingdom of God. Jesus' central message was the Gospel of the Kingdom of God, and numbered among His primary reasons for coming to Earth:

> *But He said to them, "I must preach the kingdom of God*
> *to the other cities also, for I was sent for this purpose."*
> *(Lk. 4:43)*

Further, that Gospel is eternal and unchanging *("...the ever-*
lasting gospel..." Rev. 14:6).

What is entirely overlooked by traditionalists is that gender equality comprises a key element of Jesus' Gospel, as witnessed by its prominence and frequency in Jesus' teaching and ministry, and by God's divine preservation of those testimonies in the four gospel accounts. By those virtues, gender equality therefore comprises a key element of Jesus' larger Gospel of the Kingdom of God. Accordingly, gender equality is just as unchanging and eternal an element of Jesus' Gospel as the Gospel of the Kingdom is itself everlasting and unchanging.

> **Gender equality comprises a key element of Jesus'**
> **larger, everlasting Gospel of the Kingdom of God.**

While its successful application on Earth was interrupted by the fall of man, God's original design of gender equality remains a major priority for Jesus' mission to restore all things lost by that fall.

Part of the Good News of Jesus' Gospel is that He came to set captives free, to deliver people from spiritual enslavements, to facilitate their walk in the liberty of the Spirit, and to give to them abundant *zoe*-life. This mission certainly includes the emancipation of the female half of His Kingdom citizens who have been:

- held in illegitimate bondage to mistaken extra-biblical interpretations,
- enslaved to cultural restrictions on their God-ordained ministries,
- who have been walking in stunted, spiritual half-lives in which the liberated *zoe*-life of Jesus has figuratively been choked back and unnecessarily restrained.

Consequently, there should be no Christian sexism, gender prejudice, gender bias, or gender favoritism in Jesus' true Church, precisely because God desires to bring His Kingdom and its genderless features and attributes to Earth, just as it is in Heaven.

CHAPTER 8

God Endorses Modern
Women Leaders

ANOTHER SIGNIFICANT CHALLENGE TO the Traditional
View comes, not directly from the Bible, but from the induc-
tive precedents of the leadership roles of women in both
secular and church history. Jesus said, *"...apart from Me, you
can do nothing," (Jn. 15:5).* If even one woman in modern
Christian leadership has produced authentic Kingdom fruit
in that ministry, then, according to this statement of Jesus,
it could only have been done in partnership with Jesus, and
thereby with His undeniable approval. Of course, the record
shows that multiplied thousands of women have done so,
thereby validating the Kingdom View many times over.

Further, since God Himself appoints secular governmental
leaders (cf. Rom. 13:1, John 19:10-11, Dan. 2:20-21), then
the presence of even one commendable female leader in
a secular governmental role, and generating godly results,
demonstrates His general endorsement of female leadership. Of course, the multiplicity of women in roles of secular
governmental leadership, as well as in such professional

fields as law, finance, business, medicine, science, and education, also demonstrate this point many times over.

Biblical Precedents for Extra-Biblical Illumination

The previously reviewed case of the abolition of human slavery (see Chapter 2) offers a prime example of how God has used societal influences external to Scripture itself to illuminate His truths to a resistant Church, truths that were resident in the Bible all the while, yet overlooked. However, the Bible itself contains several precedents in which extra-biblical observations were used to correct previously mistaken Christian perspectives. By extra-biblical, I refer to observations which, at the time of their original occurrence, had not yet been codified in the then-current scriptural canon. Such examples include:

- Peter's exclusive reliance upon extra-biblical, experiential, even mystical, revelations to correct the literal, if mistaken, interpretations of Jewish Christians in the church at Jerusalem (cf. Acts 11:1-16). Peter here did not cite a single scriptural passage then codified to construct his case, but instead referred to multiple mystical and extra-biblical revelations (several visions, an angelic visitation, several divine conversations, an exhibition of tongues, and a prophecy of Jesus) for his justification. In addition, I speculate that the Holy Spirit contributed His unseen influence, because Peter's case was compelling enough to correct the mistaken Jewish Christians. The extra-biblical revelations cited by Peter did not change or amend previously recorded Scripture or add any new doctrines. Rather, they illuminated the correct interpretations of previously canonized, scriptural revelations.

- The Samaritan woman at the well, who evangelized many of her neighbors using only the testimony of her personal, and distinctly mystical, encounter with Jesus (Jn. 4:5-42), rather than a scripturally based, expository explanation of the plan of salvation.

- The defense of the blind man in his trial by the Sanhedrin (cf. Jn. 9:13-41). His short, yet profound, response, *"...I was blind, but now I see..."* comprised an appeal, not to canonized scripture, but to the irrefutable, if extra-biblical and decidedly experiential fact of his own healing.

- The defense of Peter and John in their own trial before the Sanhedrin (cf. Acts 4:1-22). Like the blind man before them, their defense consisted, not of scriptural justifications, but only of their singular appeal to the experiential fact of the miraculous healing of the lame man on the steps of the Temple on the previous day (cf. Acts 3:1-8). The healing, while authentically divine, and quite factual, was nonetheless entirely experiential, and extra-biblical at the time of its occurrence.

Applying this principle to the topic of women in ministry, the countless factual testimonies of historical female leaders offer eminently compelling illumination of the truth of God's revealed logos-word, and His endorsement of their unrestricted participation in the administration of public authority over men. Co-opting the intrinsic strength of the blind man's most compelling statement, *"...I was blind, but now I see..."* I propose that thousands of women are authentically releasing the *agape*-love and *dunamis*-power of God as the minister in the name of Jesus. They are doing so as demonstrated by the collective testimony of their authentic Kingdom fruit. Therefore, God must approve of them doing so.

> If even one modern female Christian leader has produced authentic Kingdom fruit in her ministry, then it could only have been done with His endorsement and approval (cf. Jn. 15:5) ... thereby validating the Kingdom View.

If the Traditional View accurately reflected God's preference on the subject, then God would not have endorsed those countless testimonies and blessings by divinely enabling their fruition. After all, Jesus said, *"...apart from Me, you can do nothing."* (cf. Jn. 15:5). Jesus here left no room for ****** In that short statement, Jesus explicitly told us that any truly legitimate spiritual ministry can only occur in direct partnership with Him, and therefore with His implicit endorsement.

The only remaining defense available to a determined traditionalist is to then assert that every individual piece comprising the virtual mountain of spiritual fruit released by thousands of women ministers is illegitimate or fraudulent, and therefore not approved of by God. Such an assertion would necessarily be weighed against the grateful and unequivocally provable testimonies of the hundreds of thousands of beneficiaries of those ministries. In short, the transparently close-minded arrogance of such an assertion would be surpassed in its degree of offense only by its complete lack of credibility.

God's endorsement of female leaders, with their considerable authentic spiritual fruit as evidence, is demonstrated in more modern times in the following women ministers: Gladys Aylward, Corrie Ten Boom, Kathryn Kuhlman, Frances Hunter, Catherine Booth, Maria Woodworth-Etter, Aimee Semple-McPherson, Elisabeth Elliot, Ruth Graham, Ruth Ward Heflin, Beth Moore, Kay Arthur, Marilyn Hickey, Paula White, Joyce Meyer, Esther D'Conesa, Audrey Mack, Jessica Maldonado, Alice Smith, Patricia King, and Cindy Jacobs… to name but a few. Although their individual theologies and ministry styles and emphases cover a wide range, they have all first honored Jesus Christ as their Lord and Savior. And even a cursory review of their individual ministries will reveal that it would be impossible to overstate not only their authenticity, but their collective contributions to the advancement of the Kingdom of God.

A particularly committed traditionalist may be tempted here to suggest that if all the collective ministry fruit of the female ministers listed, above, is fraudulent, then it therefore poses no challenge to the Traditional View. While factually true, such critics should pursue such suggestion with the utmost care, for if it is in error, and I believe it to be so, it will place them in the very precarious and unholy danger of blaspheming the Holy Spirit by attributing His work to satan:

Whoever speaks a word against the Son of Man, it shall be forgiven him; but whoever speaks against the Holy Spirit, it shall not be forgiven him, either in this age or in the age to come. (Mt. 12:32)

Ministry Testimony of Marilyn Hickey

The example of the Christian evangelist, Marilyn A. Hickey (b. 1931), will serve in proxy for the dozens of women ministers who could be reviewed, who in turn stand in proxy for the tens of thousands of women whose ministries are less well-documented. By herself, as the keynote evangelist on the stage, Hickey has taught and preached to mixed-gender crowds of up to 300,000 people on multiple occasions in the cities of Karachi and Lahore, Pakistan. In those meetings, Hickey has been used by God to release tens of thousands of spiritual salvations and miraculous healings.

Hickey teaches the most fundamental doctrine of spiritual redemption in Christ in such an effective way that tens of thousands of people have thereby become Christians. Thousands more have been miraculously healed by the *dunamis*-power of God. These acts in the *dunamis*-power of God comprise a virtual certification of God's endorsement of her doing so. Further, to contend that she had a man present on the same stage (in the capacity of a local host pastor, or translator) as she taught and preached as the keynote speaker is so trite and superficial an accommodation to 1 Tim. 2:12 as to be immaterial to the issue at hand. God is concerned with authentic spiritual fruit, and only considers any letter-killing enslavement to mistaken interpretations for its negative impact on His priorities.

Any authentic Christian truly motivated by the *agape*-love of God would be thrilled to reproduce even a small fraction of Hickey's ministry fruit. Any authentic Christian who questions that fruit on doctrinaire grounds should seriously question their comprehension of that same love. And it is reprehensibly sad, and tragic, that anyone with far less ministry fruit would presume to sit in judgement of Hickey, on the sole basis of her gender! The literal fact of its undeniable abundance clearly validates her ministry in the eyes of God, and the legitimacy of her leadership role as a Christian woman, just as Jesus intended such fruits would do (cf. Mt. 7:18-20). If Hickey's ministry as a female were a sin in the eyes of God, God's own divine integrity would not allow Him to bless such rank disobedience. Therefore, Hickey's ministry is clearly not viewed by God as disobedience at all, but rather has been endorsed and blessed by Him as an obedient and divinely marvelous fulfillment of the Great Commission.

If God were as committed to the Traditional View as are its advocates, then the ministry testimonies of Hickey, and thousands of female ministers like her, show God to be at least inconsistent, if not irrational, or even schizophrenic, commanding gender bias in a single passage of Scripture while simultaneously and repeatedly ignoring it in His certain enablement of countless acts of ministry by women such as Hickey.

God does not change. Neither is He irrational or schizophrenic, for He is perfect (cf. Mt. 5:48). Also, His logos-word is inerrant and therefore contains no contradictions. Neither is there any credible biblical justification, dispensational or otherwise, for God perhaps allowing temporary exemptions from His revealed logos-word so that a gifted woman can temporarily fill a vacant leadership position until a suitable male could be found.

Therefore, the only reasonable interpretation one can draw from the collectively fruitful ministries of thousands of women in church history is that their disobedience to 1 Tim. 2:11-15 as alleged by the Traditional View is not disobedience at all...because the Traditional View itself is invalid. The multiplied spiritual fruit of those ministries by itself wholly invalidates the Traditional View. God is concerned with the fact that His complete Gospel is proclaimed and taught, and not the least bit concerned with the gender of those who are doing the work.

> The authentic spiritual fruit of thousands of women such as Marilyn Hickey and Beth Moore is not viewed by God as disobedience at all, rather, it validates the Kingdom View many times over.

Ministry Testimony of Alice Smith

Alice Smith, an internationally recognized deliverance minister and conference speaker, recounts the following testimony in her book, *Delivering the Captives.* The testimony describes a deliverance that she ministered to a male member of her tour group while she was accompanying her mother on a tourist trip to Israel in 1991. In the process of that ministry, Smith exercised great spiritual authority over a male, and did so with the undeniable endorsement of God.

While her tour group stopped one day at an active archeological dig of an ancient Canaanite city, a member of her group who she refers to as "Jimmy" surreptitiously picked up a very small ancient relic that was lying on the ground and put it in his pocket. Although he knew the act to be illegal, Jimmy wanted the souvenir more than he feared discovery. The relic, thousands of years old, was a very small, pagan idol made of clay.

Within minutes, Jimmy became very ill:

> Almost immediately, he became violently sick. Our director, also a medical doctor, medicated him, but two days later Jimmy was so ill that the doctor considered taking him to the hospital. (Smith, *Delivering the Captives*, pg 40)

Two days later, while the group was visiting another site in Bethlehem, Smith felt impressed by the Lord to pray for Jimmy:

> I approached Jimmy as he sat slumped in a chair, visibly miserable...
>
> I placed my hand on his forehead and softly but sternly said, "I rebuke you, spirit of infirmity, and everything attached to you, and I command you to leave this man now! I speak healing in the Name of Jesus Christ, the Messiah."
>
> The only physical manifestation in Jimmy was a noticeable shiver. (Ibid, pg 40)

Not wanting to draw any more attention...I quietly walked outside to join our group, already boarding the bus. Within a few minutes, Jimmy and his wife came rushing out in tears. He grabbed me in his arms and cried, "I'm healed, I'm healed!" Everyone, including our Jewish tour guide, gasped in amazement. (Ibid, pg 40)

Later that day, I visited Jimmy and his wife in their hotel room. When I asked if the Lord had revealed the source of the sickness, Jimmy said yes, it had been the small idol he'd placed in his pocket. After his deliverance in Bethlehem, he crushed the clay object under his feet. I prayed with both of them and advised Jimmy to repent of what he'd done and to break any lingering attachment it might have on his life. A curse had been placed on him through this forbidden object, and he knew it. I occasionally see him, and he reports he's not had a problem since. (Ibid, pg. 41)

Jimmy was certainly thankful that day that Smith did not allow gender restrictions on her ministry (such as Dr. No would zealously impose) to prohibit her ministry of deliverance to those of the opposite gender.

Women in Prominent, Secular Leadership Roles

Scripture reveals that God appoints secular governmental leaders, and history demonstrates that the leaders He so appoints are sometimes females.

Every person is to be in subjection to the governing authorities. For there is no authority except from God, and those which exist are established by God. (Rom. 13:1. See also John 19:10-11, Dan 2:20-21).

Such appointments by themselves demonstrate that God preferentially favors neither gender for such roles. If God preferred only male leaders, the fact that He promotes female leaders in secular arenas, in even a single instance, by itself legitimizes the Kingdom View.

If Rom. 13:1 is true, and God appoints female governmental leaders, then the repeated reality of female governmental leaders by itself legitimizes the Kingdom View.

The following list of prominent female leaders in secular positions of high authority or significant accomplishment offers confirmation that God exhibits no gender bias in the secular governmental leaders He appoints. At its most fundamental level, this is because both genders were created in the image of God, and women in general are therefore just as capable as men of leading and managing organizations of every size and function:

- Susan B. Anthony – American social reformer and women's rights activist,
- Rosa Parks – American civil rights activist,
- Golda Meir – Prime Minister of Israel, 1969-1974,
- Margaret Thatcher – Prime Minister of the United Kingdom, 1979-1990,
- Condoleezza Rice–US Secretary of State, 2005-2009,

- Michele Bachmann – US Congresswoman, 2007-2015,
- Nimrata "Nikki" Haley – Governor of South Carolina, U.S. Ambassador to the United Nations, S.C. State Representative, 2005-2018,
- Amy Coney Barrett – Associate Justice, Supreme Court of USA – 2020-Present.

The preceding list offers only sufficient illustration of the reality that God has included women in His appointments of positions of high secular authority or accomplishment. And if this is true for women in secular roles, how much more true it will be if their natural abilities are informed and guided by the indwelling Holy Spirit as they minister in the name of Jesus Christ, within the Church at large. And if God has not excluded women from such roles, then neither should Christians.

CHAPTER 9

Male Dominance in the Bible is Not What it Seems

SEVERAL MISBELIEFS SOMETIMES CITED to support the Traditional View include the following:

- Most church leaders in the New Testament were men, and this gender bias reflects God's preference both then and now.
- Gender differences in physical and psychological attributes of males compared to females favor male leadership.

While based only on inference and observation, and lacking any explicit biblical support, these two misbeliefs are nonetheless common to those advocating the Traditional View of women in the Kingdom of God.

Most Church Leaders in the New Testament Were Men

Traditionalists routinely assert that God's preferences for male leaders is indicated by the genders of all the original twelve apostles, all personally chosen by Jesus Himself, and all of whom were males. While factually true, the implication that these choices support the Traditional View is false.

This apparent gender bias by Jesus should not be interpreted as gender favoritism by God for its own sake. Rather, it reflects God's accommodation of the cultural realities present in that part of the world in that day, rather than His eternal prejudice. God made this accommodation because Jesus' acceptance as a rabbi among the Jews depended on His having at least ten male disciples. Any women in Jesus' core group of twelve apostles would have not only not been recognized as legitimate disciples by His very sexist Jewish critics, but would also have severely damaged His credibility in their eyes.

That God might make such an allowance does not reflect any weakness or compromise on His part. However, it does reflect His supreme wisdom in presenting His Gospel in the most palatable packaging possible, while not compromising its integrity. Such accommodation on the part of God is also observed in other features of God's Gospel presentation to men.

That Jesus' choice of only male apostles was an accommodation only, and not a valid doctrinal precedent, is made even more apparent by the fact that He also chose only Jewish males of local Palestinian origin who were probably between 15 and 30 years of age and spoke Aramaic, and probably Hebrew. Such candidates would be much more likely to be accepted by the local population than Jews of foreign birth, and certainly more so than Gentile candidates. That most modern Christians recognize that the male gender of Jesus' apostles was merely an accommodation by God is readily revealed by observing that no modern church also requires that its pastors, leaders, elders, etc., in addition to being males, also be Jewish Palestinians, between 15 and 30 years of age, and fluent in Aramaic and Hebrew.

That Father God might so accommodate the prejudices of mere mortals may seem unnecessary in view of His omnipotence, but the reality is that He has done so many times. In what is perhaps the most profound such accommodation of all, God chose to deliver His Gospel to men in the form of an ordinary human named Jesus. God could have delivered the same news through any number of magnificently spectacular means, complete with supernatural special effects. For example, He could have had the arch-angel Michael, floating in the sky, broadcast the news through heavenly loudspeakers, through clouds of thunder and bolts of lightning, supported by a heavenly choral host that was shouting a thunderous "Amen" after each declaration. Or He could have had a fully adult Jesus simply appear on the steps of the temple in Jerusalem, sling a few Tesla-bolts from His fingertips, slap down a fully composed New Testament written on leaves of gold, and then levitate back up to Heaven. After all, a pre-incarnate Jesus had appeared to men in an adult form multiple times before His human birth in Bethlehem, such as to Abraham at the oasis of Mamre (cf. Gen. 18:1-3), to Jacob in a wrestling match (cf. Gen. 32:24-34), and to Shadrach, Meshach, and Abednego in their fiery ordeal (cf. Dan. 3:25).

Precisely as an accommodation to the prejudices of ordinary men, however, God delivered the Gospel to mankind in the most accommodating form possible, through that of an ordinary man, Jesus, first entering the world as an ordinary baby, born to a mother like every other man. And God did so precisely to make His Gospel as palatable as possible to a skeptical and tradition-bound audience who had more than enough free will to reject it.

Other, much less profound examples of God's accommodation include the fact that Jesus' first ministry was to the Jews, a group who would have adamantly rejected not only any female apostles, but also any gentile members of the core group of twelve. This reality is underscored by other accommodations, such as the fact that each of the chosen twelve was also an adult Jew who spoke Hebrew and probably also Aramaic, other requirements for their initial ministry to Jews.

Therefore, the male gender of the original twelve apostles reflects just another accommodation by God, rather than a doctrinally inviolable reflection of His preference for male leaders.

Do Their Physical and Psychological Attributes Favor Male Leadership?

While they do not comprise biblical justifications, the distinct physiological and psychological differences between men and women are sometimes cited to support the Traditional View.

For example, for many centuries the established patriarchal centers of authority and political power considered women to have insufficient intelligence to become educated, to run businesses, to manage governmental affairs, or to serve in various roles of Church leadership. And the notion has been reinforced over the centuries by institutionalized, if confused, circular logic and confirmation bias. Incredible though it may have been, the lack of educated women by itself was used, if illogically so, to support the contention that women were therefore less intelligent and less able to be educated.

However, neither gender is intrinsically smarter than the other. Objective modern studies have consistently shown there are no meaningful differences in intelligence between adult men and women.

> **Neither gender is intrinsically smarter than the other: objective modern studies have consistently shown that there are no meaningful differences in intelligence between adult men and women.**

It is widely recognized that young females tend to develop mentally at a faster pace than males, as most parents have observed. Most parents recognize, for example, that girls will learn to speak much sooner than boys, and will commonly use a far larger vocabulary at a similar young age. And since vocabulary is a universally recognized bellwether of basic intelligence, one could suggest that this observation indicates girls are smarter than boys at the same young age. Other research has revealed multiple related differences between the sexes:

While still in their mothers' wombs, boy babies have much more testosterone in their bodies than girl babies, and this testosterone directly affects the development of their brains. For example, boys tend to perceive colors at the blue end of the spectrum more easily while girls tend to perceive colors at the red end of the spectrum more easily. Boys as a group prefer to engage in task-oriented projects, while girls tend to perform better at multi-tasking. The region of the brain that helps control language and emotion – called the caudate – tends to be larger in girls, as does that part of the brain (the larger corpus callosum), that connects the two sides of the brain.

Abridged from online article by Woolston, Chris; *Brain development: Is the difference between boys and girls all in their heads?*

However, males gain intelligence parity with females by adulthood. All modern research indicates that any gender-based differences in their relative intelligence in infancy and adolescence become negligible in adult populations. Therefore, there is no credible justification for prejudice in Christian ministry based only on the relative intelligence of each gender.

Relative Emotional Expressivity

Regarding the trait of emotional expressivity, some have argued that women are more emotionally expressive, and are therefore less qualified to be leaders on that basis alone. While the Bible nowhere makes this recommendation, it does specify the gender-neutral requirements that leaders should be both self-controlled while also being not quick-tempered (cf. Tit. 1:7-9). It is critical to note that these are issues of character rather than gender since each gender is equally capable of violating both requirements. In my personal experience, it is no more or less likely that a female leader will be overly expressive than a male leader will be too quick-tempered, for example. Any leadership decision unduly influenced by uncontrolled emotions, whether the offense is excessive empathy or free-range anger, can potentially lead to error, without regard to the gender of the offending leader.

In addition, emotional suppression can be every bit as dangerous in a leader as excessive emotional expression. Assume, only for the sake of this discussion, that women are more emotionally expressive than men. If so, then it is necessarily true, by default, that men are correspondingly more emotionally suppressive than women….and either extreme on that spectrum is a dangerous trait in a ministry leader. Suppression of emotions in no way guarantees that the suppressed emotions won't affect a decision despite their superficial suppression. It is highly likely that such suppressed emotions will have some impact, perhaps even adversely so, upon a person's judgement even if he is unaware of the effect. Further, suppressed emotions have the annoying habit of later surfacing in very counterproductive, even damaging, outbursts if they are not adequately addressed.

The the considerable internal stresses that often accrue to roles of Christian leadership will be just as potentially destructive and debilitating to a female leader who might be overly expressive as to a male leader who might be overly suppressive. In both cases, transparent honesty with one-self, consistent prayer, confession and forgiveness, spiritual deliverance, and counseling when appropriate, are gen-der-neutral enablements of which every leader, regardless of their gender, should avail themselves as the needs arise.

Further, a lack of empathy and emotional transparency, as well as undue suppression of those responses, can easily lead to unnecessary misunderstanding, conflict, division, and even catastrophic confrontation. The case is easily made that, in such cases, had there been more empathy, more emotional transparency, and yes, even more emotional expressivity, any resulting conflict could have been either mitigated ahead of a crisis, or avoided altogether.

In summary, no one, whether male or female, should be appointed as a leader if their character traits are insuffi-cient to meet the challenges of the role. However, the Bible nowhere recommends a bias on the sole basis of gen-der-based distinctions regarding emotional tendencies.

> If women are assumed to be more emotionally expres-sive than men, then it is necessarily true that men are correspondingly more emotionally suppressive than women....and either extreme on that spectrum is a dangerous trait in any leader.

Physiological Differences

Regarding physiological differences between males and females, those few times in which specific physical demands of a circumstance in ministry might make any material difference in its effectiveness are so rare in modern times as to comprise mere anecdotes. Therefore, they hardly qualify as a credible foundation to limit women in ministry.

Relative physical strength, for example, may determine victory in a sports contest or a military conflict, and men, in general, are taller, stronger, faster, and have more stamina than women. This reality is reflected in the fact that Olympic sports are segregated by gender, with the male athletes having superior performances. However, success in spiritual contests is far more often determined by spiritual factors such as knowledge, faith, hope, and love, factors that are unrelated to brute strength, physical endurance, or pain threshold. Average males could arguably carry more Bibles or medical supplies on their own backs over a range of mountains or through a tropical jungle than average females. However, even if such circumstances sometimes exist in today's modern world, not only are they extremely rare, but they are more than offset by satellite phones, off-road vehicles, bush pilots, pack animals, and human porters. Accordingly, they fall woefully short of having sufficient collective merit to provide any basis for generalized Christian sexism across the Church at large, and certainly not within any church in any but the most remote and inaccessible geographical settings.

Beyond physical strength and stature, women typically live longer than men. Rather than a detriment, however, their longer lives automatically afford women proportionately more time to accumulate knowledge, wisdom, and experience, and to grow in faith and love. If anything, therefore, such attributes should make older women, at least, proportionately better equipped to be church leaders and teachers than men.

The one category of ministry which may deserve some gender distinction is that of evangelism to heavily patriarchal, pagan cultures. A male evangelist may be more readily received in such cultures than a female. However, God in His infinite wisdom is the One who calls evangelists to serve, and then assigns to them their areas of service. And He has chosen women to evangelize such cultures in the past (e.g., the Samaritan woman who evangelized her town (cf. Jn. 4:7-42), so such assignments and callings should be reserved for God alone.

The gender differences mentioned above are real enough. Rather than serving as limitations on women in Christian ministry, however, they comprise elements of a divinely orchestrated system of mutually beneficial co-dependencies written into the very fabric of human existence by Father God. These differences comprise gender-based strengths and weaknesses that are so complementary that neither gender functions optimally without the participating strengths of the other.

> God has promised to supernaturally enable each of us, both males and females, to perform the ministries for which He has chosen us, and to release the spiritual gifts He has sovereignly given to us. If God appoints someone to be a leader, He has not done so in error, or in ignorance of his perceived shortcomings...God does not make mistakes.

God has generally designed men and women to communicate with words, to be emotional beings, and to exert ourselves physically and emotionally in His service. In addition, He has also promised to supernaturally enable every Christian, both male or female, to perform the specific ministries for which He has chosen us, and to release the spiritual gifts He has sovereignly given to each of us.

The Kingdom reality is that the more closely that each leader becomes transformed into the image of Christ in every aspect of his life, the less any personal shortcomings will affect his service to the Kingdom of God. The character traits of Jesus and spiritual fruit that every Christian is to strive to emulate (ref. the fruit of the Spirit in Gal. 5:22-23) are uniformly gender-neutral, because Jesus' character has no distinctly feminine or masculine traits, only Godly traits. Both men and women are equally enjoined to demonstrate and release righteousness, love, joy, peace, patience, kindness, goodness, faithfulness, gentleness, and self-control. And as the New Testament makes abundantly clear, any leader qualified by the Bible's high standards for Christian leadership will already be well advanced along the gender-neutral path to Christlikeness in his personal character (e.g., 1 Tim. 3:1-13, Tit. 1:5-9, 1 Cor. 6:9-10).

If God appoints or calls a person to be a Christian leader, He has not done so in error, or in ignorance of the person's perceived shortcomings: God neither makes mistakes, nor fumbles along with intentions having coincidental or haphazard consequences. Both the Bible and church history are clear that God has deliberately chosen women as well as men to lead His people. Equally compelling is that no single human image within the Body of Christ is any less an authentic image of God than any other on the sole basis of its gender. Accordingly, there are no psychological or physiological differences between males and females that justify any Christian sexism or gender bias in roles of Christian leadership in the true Church of Jesus Christ.

CHAPTER 10

Final Thoughts

THE PRECEDING CHAPTERS EACH reviewed different aspects of the ongoing awakening of women in Christian ministry, the two opposing views on its biblical legitimacy, and their relative biblical justifications. This short chapter offers a very brief summary of the justifications for the view favored by this book, the Kingdom View. It then offers further illumination of those justifications with a short series of rhetorical questions. Finally, it frames the entire subject by the ministry experience of a single female pastor now in active service to God in the country of Zaire.

A Brief List of the Main Justifications for the Kingdom View

Any simplistic reading of biblical passages in support of the Traditional View must be reconciled with the following, biblically based observations:

1. The primary passage cited to support the Traditional View (1 Tim. 3:1-15) is demonstrated to have a more accurate interpretation that invalidates that support,

2. The eight more secondary passages cited to support the Traditional View are demonstrated to have better, alternate interpretations that invalidate that support,

3. There are no gender distinctions in the Heavenly Kingdom of God (e.g., Garden of Eden, the Millennial Kingdom, or Heaven), so there should therefore be no gender distinctions in any expression of the Kingdom of God on Earth,

4. The spiritual offices and gifts, given "for the common good," include no gender restrictions or distinctions. If a woman is given an authentic spiritual gift of teaching, for example, we can be certain that it was given for "the common good," a range of beneficiaries that includes both genders, and not just for the common good of women under their authority,

5. The prophet Joel, later confirmed by the apostle Peter, prophesied that women (and men) would prophesy during the Church age (Joel 2:28, Acts 2:18),

6. David prophesied that a "great host" of women would proclaim Jesus' Gospel (Ps. 68:11), another confirmation of Joel's prophecy in Joel 2:28,

7. Paul, in full confirmation of Joel's prophecy, specifically authorized women to pray and prophesy in public church meetings (1 Cor. 11:5),

8. Both Jesus and Paul told all Christians, including women, to teach and disciple (Mt. 28:18-20, Col. 3:16),

9. The royal priesthood that comprises the Body of Christ comprises both genders (1 Pet. 2:5-9),

10. Both genders share equal spiritual status in the Body of Christ (Mt. 23:1-12),

11. God has endorsed women teaching men, judging them, leading them, and exercising *exousia*-authority

over them in the Old Testament, with the following women as witnesses: Miriam, Huldah, Deborah, and Esther,

12. God has endorsed women teaching men, judging them, leading them, and exercising *exousia*-authority over them in the New Testament, with the following women as witnesses: Anna, Junia, Phoebe, four prophetic daughters of Phillip, Priscilla, as well as eleven other women,

13. God has endorsed women teaching men, prophesying over them, and exercising *exousia*-authority over them in recent church history, with Beth Moore and Marilyn Hickey as lead witnesses and proxies for thousands of others,

14. God has elevated and endorsed women leaders in secular arenas of politics, finance, law, business, and education, offering another demonstration of His lack of gender bias for women in leadership roles,

15. Jesus' own emancipation of women confirms the Kingdom View;

16. Paul explicitly confirmed that in Christ, within the Kingdom of God on Earth, there are no gender distinctions (cf. Gal. 3:26-29),

17. God confirms that He loves men and women equally as His spiritual children (2 Cor. 6:18);

18. Since a majority of the original twelve apostles had no formal education, the fact that most women of Jesus' day had no formal education offers no credible reason to prohibit them from teaching men, either then or now,

19. The Kingdom View fosters spiritual liberty and full zoe-life in the Body of Christ, whereas the Traditional

View fosters spiritual bondage and stunted, hamstrung spiritual growth,

20. The number of harvest workers in the fields of Christian service and missions are few enough that it is demonstrably and woefully counterproductive, even satanically so, to tell those who also happen to be female, to "go home and be silent" on the sole basis of their gender,

21. God is well able to lead, guide, and enable females as well as males. Therefore, any rejection or devaluation of divine enablement in females based only on their gender comprises a virtual rejection or devaluation of the God (and Holy Spirit) who divinely authored their ordination and enablement,

22. This Women's Awakening comprises a vital part of God's ongoing restoration of the larger, complete Gospel of the Kingdom of God across the full breadth of Jesus' Church around the world.

A Few Direct Questions

Regarding how the information in this book should apply to the modern Body of Christ, the following questions have been posed and answered to further emphasize the key points of this book.

Question 1: Should the Body of Christ exile the collective God-given contributions, insights and considerable spiritual fruit of spiritually gifted women to a rebellious, disobedient fringe of Christianity, solely on the doctrinaire grounds of a mistaken interpretation of a single verse (1 Tim. 2:12)?

The biblically correct answer is a resounding "no," because it is the compelling testimony of both the Bible and established biblical history that God gives spiritual gifts equally to both men and women. It is further demonstrated that all such gifts, regardless of the gender of their chosen recipient, are given for the common good of the Church...not just for those of the same gender. In addition, God correspondingly approves of and endorses women in every leadership and teaching position within the Body of Christ.

Question 2: Were the thousands of salvations and miraculous healings, released through female ministers, as they have taught and ministered with men in their audiences, merely the counterfeit signs of false teachers and prophets, and illegitimate by reason of their gender alone?

The biblically correct answer is, "no," for they have universally glorified God, and Jesus was quite clear that satan will not sponsor any miraculous works that do so.

Question 3: Should women be allowed to author books, Christian music, and Bible studies on spiritual topics, and should Christian men then be allowed to read, sing, and study them, respectively?

The biblically correct answer is, "yes," because God has imparted much divine wisdom to women, has placed no related, gender-based restrictions on the ministry activities of women, and the entire Church is in desperate need of all such contributions.

Question 4: Should a woman be allowed to lead a general congregation in prayer from the pulpit, or serve as its worship leader, or as a member of a worship team, without direct oversight by a man?

The biblically correct answer is, "yes," because God has anointed many women for such roles, empowered them to so minister, and has placed no related restrictions on the ministry activities of women on the sole basis of their gender.

Question 5: Should the Church permit a woman to be an apostle, prophet, teacher, senior pastor, evangelist, bishop, elder, or deacon, and thereby be given spiritual authority over men in a congregation, without direct oversight by a man?

The biblically correct answer is, "yes," because multiple biblical precedents have clearly endorsed and established women with such authority over men.

Question 6: Could it possibly be in the heart of God for men to simply quote 1 Tim. 2:11-15 as a proof text, tell every woman leader and teacher to "go home," and then hope and pray that a man will then arise to fill those empty shoes, and share the same insights, wisdom, testimonies, revelations, and ministries?

The biblically correct answer is, "no," because there are no ministry-based gender distinctions in either the New Testament Church or the Kingdom of God. Consequently, there should therefore be no such distinctions in the Church of Jesus Christ. The workers really are few, as Jesus told us, and the modern Church desperately needs every leader and teacher, regardless of their gender, to release every gift, insight, exhortation and point of direction imparted to them.

In conclusion, a fully balanced interpretation of all the justifications discussed in the preceding chapters clearly demonstrates that God has released women to minister in every role and capacity as men, both inside and outside of His Church, specifically including holding spiritual authority over, and teaching, men.

Testimony of the Spiritual Power of a Female Witness and Minister

The following account testifies of the *agape*-love and *dunamis*-power that God is eager to release through either men or women who are bold enough to be His vessels. Its female protagonist was bold enough to proclaim Jesus' Gospel, despite mistaken scriptural prohibitions and traditional cultural taboos. For background context, significant cultural gender oppression exists in the indigenous societal cultures of modern Zaire, as in so many other places in today's world.

> Some years ago, Mahesh (Chavda) was holding evangelistic meetings in Kinshasa, Zaire. A woman who was dying of gangrene poisoning and paralyzed from the waist down was brought across the river from Brazzaville to Kinshasa to the meeting. That night, lying on a stretcher in the midst of the crowd, she raised her hand and recited the sinner's prayer, receiving Jesus in her heart. At that moment, the healing power of the risen Christ went through her entire body and

healed her of paralysis and gangrene. She jumped off the stretcher and started leaping up and down, giving thanks to God.

Several years later, Mahesh returned to the region, holding leaders' meetings and evangelistic outreaches. On one day he took a brief tour of the fishing village of Oveira. As he was ministering among the poor at the river, a woman ran up to Mahesh, calling him "Papa." This woman, who was obviously well-known to all those around her, was the same dying, paralyzed woman who had traveled to Kinshasa for a miracle a few years earlier. She had received her drink of the living water that springs up to eternal life and, like the Samaritan woman at Jacob's well, had returned to her city bearing the good news of the Gospel. In the several years since, she had raised up an entire church and ministry in Oveira, with the Lord working mightily in signs and wonders the whole time.

She had come for a drink and a healing: she received an ocean of inheritance, destiny, promise, anointing, and purpose for her life and the lives of others. (Chavda, *The Hidden Power of a Woman*, pg 36, emphasis mine).

Jesus' own version of His Gospel authentically recognizes no sexist distinctions in who qualifies as its leaders, and therefore those who proclaim that Gospel to the ends of the Earth should be likewise unconstrained. It takes no imagination to speculate how the woman in the preceding testimony might respond if told by Dr. No that she should "go home" solely because of his so firmly expressed opinions.

Without her knowledge or consultation, I have taken the speculative liberty of ghostwriting for the woman in the testimony what I consider to be a respectful, yet stern, response to attitudes like those of Dr. No (see Chapter 2). Like the Samaritan woman at the well, or the blind man in front of the Sanhedrin, she would be divinely justified in making the following statement to anyone attacking her from the same antagonistically legalistic perspective as that of Dr. No:

> "You have a sterile, death-by-letter, gender-biased doctrine, but I have a healed body, a living church and a Spirit-filled ministry. Jesus saved my spirit and healed my body, not your zoe-toxic doctrine. I am too excited and engaged in proclaiming His complete Gospel to remain silent, and am only encouraged by God's obvious and continuing endorsement of my ministry through its multiplied salvations, miracles, signs, and wonders. By all means, assemble a sympathetic audience, solicit a few laughs, harrumph a few times, and reassure their insecurities and your own with the dogmatic arrogance and brutish insensitivity displayed by your comments. You certainly have the freedom to prosecute the issue all you like, in front of a rigged kangaroo court of opinion, in an echo-chamber of your choosing and design.
>
> However, like you, I also have the freedom in God to respond to His specific calling on my own life. I do not require either your permission or validation to do

so. Therefore, you will excuse me, you must excuse me...in fact, you will be unable to constrain me, while I continue, as a woman ordained by God Himself, to proclaim the complete Gospel of the Kingdom of God, to both women and men, as He leads me.

Period, paragraph, end of discussion."

Bibliography

Cambridge Online Dictionary, https://dictionary.cambridge.org/us/dictionary/english/sexism

Celoria, Heather; *Does 1 Timothy 2 Prohibit Women from Teaching, Leading, and Speaking in the Church?* https://www.cbeinternational.org/resources/article/priscilla-papers, accessed on Dec. 17, 2019.

Chavda, Mahesh; *The Hidden Power of a Woman.* Destiny Image Publishers, Shippensburg, PA, 2006

The Passion Translation; Passion & Fire Ministries, Inc., Broadstreet Publishing Group, LLC, Savage, MN, Copyright 2017, 2018

May, G.Y. and Joe, H.P.: *Setting the Record Straight,* http://www.cbeinternational.org/?q=content/setting-record-straight-response-ji-packers-position-womens-ordination)

Merriam-Webster, *Online Dictionary*: https://www.merriam-webster.com/

Renner, Rick; *Home Group – Women in Ministry, Jan 5, 2015,* https://www.youtube.com/watch?v=Ju-nxjV5jaE, accessed on Dec 28. 2019.

Smith, Alice; *Delivering the Captives*. Bethany House, Grand Rapids, MI, 2006

Sutterer, Dr. Kent, as reported by "Breakthrough 2019," https://www.historyvshollywood.com/reelfaces/breakthrough, accessed on Feb. 20, 2020.

Thomas, Dalton; filmmaker of documentary, *Sheep Among Wolves*, interview with the Christian Broadcasting Network on August 2019. https://www.youtube.com/watch?v=rXLjwFdr4eU, accessed on March 31, 2020.

Young, Allison; *1 Timothy 2:11-15*, http://www.cbeinternational.org/?q=content/1-timothy-211-15, accessed on July 7, 2021

Woolston, Chris; *Brain development: Is the difference between boys and girls all in their heads?*, www.babycenter.com, accessed on March 2, 2021

Companion Books in
This Series*

THE SUBJECT OF THIS book is such good news that it qualifies as a limited gospel in its own right. This is a particularly appropriate perspective, given that it came into being as a part of the author's continuing investigation of a far more extensive subject, that of Jesus' own version of the Gospel of the Kingdom of God.

Referring to Jesus' "own version" of His Gospel in that way implies that there are other, alternate versions that are competing for the attention and reverence of Christians. This provocative assertion will interest many, while offending others. In every case, however, it is my prayer that it will lead every honest investigator to fall ever more fully in love with Father God, and to rededicate his life to seeking first His Kingdom.

Referring to Jesus' "own version" of His Gospel implies that there are other, alternate versions that are competing with it for the attention and reverence of modern Christians. By alternate versions, I am referring, not to the widely divergent and corrupted versions promoted by cults or false religions, but to seemingly orthodox versions advocated by mainstream Christian sects and denominations. This provocative assertion will interest many but offend others. Regardless of one's reaction to that assertion, the goal of this series of books is to demonstrate that Jesus' own version of His Gospel differs in several critical aspects from the alternate versions being taught to millions of modern Christians, and Jesus' true Church desperately needs to rediscover and proclaim Jesus' own version.

In the case of this volume, God's liberation of women is closely aligned with God's liberation of many other types of captives through the compassion, love, and power of Jesus' larger Gospel of the Kingdom of God. Correspondingly, many other marvelous aspects of Jesus' Gospel can serve to spiritually supercharge not only women, but men as well, in their ministries after their liberation from a wide variety of captivities. Many of these other aspects will be discussed soon in the following books, all of which comprise distinctly complementary companions to this volume:

Vol. 1: *Jesus' Gospel of the Kingdom of God: Foundations*
Rediscovering Jesus' Own Version of His Gospel

Vol. 2: *Jesus' Gospel of the Kingdom of God: Key Identities*
How You Should Relate to God, Jesus, and Holy Spirit

Vol. 3: *Jesus' Gospel of the Kingdom of God: A Woman's Place*
There is no Sexism in Jesus' Gospel

Vol. 4: *Jesus' Gospel of the Kingdom of God: Obstructions*
* *Church-imposed Restrictions on the Kingdom of God*

Vol 5: *Jesus' Gospel of the Kingdom of God: Living in Victory*
Walking and Serving in Relationship with Jesus

*anticipated publication by year-end 2022.

9 781662 831799